MW00881023

THIS BOOK BELONGS TO:

....

IT WAS GIVEN TO ME BY:

....

ON:

....

3-MINUTE
BEDtime
PRAYERS

FOR BOYS

JANICE THOMPSON

BARBOUR kidz
A Division of Barbour Publishing

Print ISBN 978-1-63609-639-1

Published by Barbour Publishing, Inc., 1810 Barbour Drive, Uhrichsville, Ohio 44683, www.barbourbooks.com.

Our mission is to inspire the world with the life-changing message of the Bible.

Member of the
Evangelical Christian
Publishers Association

Printed in China.

001694   0823   HA

May these words of mine, which I have prayed to the Lord, be near to the Lord our God day and night.
1 Kings 8:59

INTRODUCTION

Sometimes you come to the end of a long day and you just want to crawl into bed, pull the covers up to your chin, and forget about all of the rough things that happened.

But before you drift off, don't forget to spend some time with Jesus. Thank Him for helping you through another day. Praise Him for all He's doing in your life. And let Him know that you trust Him—even with the big stuff you don't understand.

In this inspiring prayer book you'll find 180 nighttime prayers that will help you draw closer to your heavenly Father—the one who created you and knows you best.

- First, take a minute to read the scripture verse.

- Then pray the prayer. . .from your heart.

- Finally, take a moment to think about what you've just read. God wants you to learn from this little book!

Your heavenly Father loves you most. You can trust Him, even while you sleep. Remember, He never falls asleep on the job!

YOU MADE IT ALL

*In the beginning God made from nothing
the heavens and the earth.*
GENESIS 1:1

You're amazing, Lord God! You must have the best imagination ever! You made everything out of absolutely nothing. (How did You do that?) The world was like a blank piece of paper with nothing written on it, and You looked at it and wrote a whole story. And You made me part of that story. Thank You so much for being our amazing Creator! You were creating then, and You're creating now. You're always making everything new, and I'm so glad. Tonight as I snuggle into bed, I want to thank You for all You've created. Amen.

———— THINK ABOUT IT: ————

If your teacher asked you to complete a science project, you couldn't start with nothing, could you? God started from nothing and made everything! He's the only one who could do that.

Let There Be Light

Then God said, "Let there be light," and there was light.
GENESIS 1:3

How did You do it, Lord God? How did You look into the darkness and speak a few words. . .and everything changed? You said, "Let there be light!" and—bam!—light appeared. Crazy bright light that drove the darkness away! That's amazing. Your words changed everything during creation, and they're changing things now too. Thank You for speaking good words over my life! You're creating great things in me, and I'm so grateful for Your power! Amen.

THINK ABOUT IT:

If God's words were powerful enough to create the sun, moon, and stars and keep them in place, isn't He powerful and trustworthy enough to take care of you, even while you're asleep?

yes

THE DIVIDING LINE

God saw that the light was good.
He divided the light from the darkness.
GENESIS 1:4

Father God, as soon as You created the light, You looked at it and said, "That's good!" And it's *still* good. There's a lot of dark (bad) stuff in this world, and You're always telling me, "Stay away from that dark stuff—it's not good for you!" So I will. I'll stay on the light side of things. I won't mess with lying, cheating, and hurting others. I want to live in the light every single day, because I know it makes You glad! I messed up a few times today, but You can help me do better tomorrow. Amen.

THINK ABOUT IT:

God took the time to divide the light from
the dark. That means there's an obvious
separation between the two. How can you
be sure to walk in the light each day?

think before you do it

ONLY YOU, GOD

"Have no gods other than Me."
EXODUS 20:3

Sometimes I read this verse and wonder what You mean, Lord. You're the only true God, after all! Then I remember that sometimes I make other things more important than You. Friendships. Grades. Talents. Possessions. I spend a lot of time thinking about those things instead of focusing on You. Thanks for reminding me that You are the most important thing in my life—You, and only You. I won't put anything ahead of You, Jesus! Tomorrow is a fresh, new day, and I will do my best with Your help. Amen.

--- **THINK ABOUT IT:** ---

Is there anything in your life that you put ahead of Jesus? Friendships? Sports? Possessions? Tonight, before you go to sleep, ask Him to forgive you, and start fresh tomorrow.

A STRANGE WAY TO CREATE

Then the Lord God made man from the dust of the ground. And He breathed into his nose the breath of life. Man became a living being.
GENESIS 2:7

Father God, You chose a strange way to create men and women! You picked up some dust and breathed into it? Out of the dust came a man? Then You took a rib from the man while he was sleeping and turned it into a woman? You're a creative God! If You could do all of that (turning dust and a rib into humans), then I know I can count on You to turn the not-so-great situations in my life around. You are amazing at re-creating! Tonight while I'm sleeping, I'll trust You with my problems, large and small. Amen.

THINK ABOUT IT:

God makes good things out of bad. And He never changes—so He's still turning bad into good! Do you trust Him to fix the tough stuff in your life?

yes

YOU ARE SPIRIT

"God is Spirit. Those who worship Him must worship Him in spirit and in truth."
JOHN 4:24

Sometimes I try to imagine what You look like, Lord God. I wonder if You have eyes and hair and hands and feet. Then I remember that the Bible says You are Spirit. Until I get to heaven, I won't ever see You face-to-face, but I can sense Your presence near me, even when I'm sleeping. I don't have to see You to trust You. I don't have to touch You to know You're there. You're right here with me, even now, as I climb into bed and chill out for a good night's sleep. I trust You, my heavenly Father!

--------- **THINK ABOUT IT:** ---------

Do you have to "see" the wind to know it's blowing? Do you have to "see" the water in the pipes to know it will come out when you turn on the faucet?

YOU ARE THE ONLY WAY

Jesus said, "I am the Way and the Truth and the Life. No one can go to the Father except by Me."
JOHN 14:6

Some days I just don't know which way to go. I make wrong decisions and end up sorry for them. But You always help me correct my course so I can go in the right direction again. You're great with directions, Jesus! You lead and guide me all the way. I love this promise from Your Word. It says that You are the Way, the Truth, and the Life. (No wonder You're so great at guiding me!) You show me the way every single time. I'm so grateful! Amen.

—————— **THINK ABOUT IT:** ——————

Jesus is the only way to get to heaven. If He knows how to get you to heaven, doesn't He surely know how to guide you in your life?

YOU ARE THE FIRST AND LAST

*"I am the First and the Last. I am
the beginning and the end."*
REVELATION 22:13

Jesus, You are the first and the last, the beginning and the end. My day starts and ends with You. And You are there for every single moment in between. You're there when I'm in school, wishing I didn't have to be. You're there when I'm arguing with my dad. (Ugh!) You're right there when I'm trying to figure out how to do my homework. You're even there when my little brother is doing his best to annoy me. I'm so happy You're always with me, Jesus. Amen.

—————— THINK ABOUT IT: ——————

If Jesus created everything and is the beginning
and ending of everything, doesn't it make sense
that He's always there when you need Him?

YOU DO IMPOSSIBLE THINGS

Jesus said, "God can do things men cannot do."
LUKE 18:27

I could give You a whole list of things that I don't know how to do, Lord God. Some things feel impossible to me. I try and try and just can't figure everything out. But You can do everything! You do impossible things. You tell storms to stop. . .and they do. You tell hearts to beat. . .and they do. You heal the sick, fix broken relationships, and even calm people down when they get mad. (I know, because You've done this for me when I couldn't do it myself.) There's *nothing* You can't do. So I'm going to trust You to do everything I can't. Amen.

THINK ABOUT IT:

If God could create the whole universe,
isn't He able to work other miracles too?

YOU NEVER CHANGE

*Jesus Christ is the same yesterday
and today and forever.*
HEBREWS 13:8

Today I woke up in my pajamas. Then I changed into my clothes. Then I changed back into some pajamas. Some days I change into a sports uniform or swim trunks. I change, change, change. And my attitude changes too. Some days I'm happy; other days I'm sad. Some days I'm a hard worker; other days I'm lazy. Some days I say nice things to my family; other days I'm rude to them. (I change all the time!) I'm so glad You're an unchanging God! You're always the same loving heavenly Father, no matter what.

——————— **THINK ABOUT IT:** ———————

God loved you even before you were born.
If He's the same yesterday, today, and forever,
don't you think He'll go on loving you forever?

I PRAISE YOU IN GOOD TIMES AND BAD

Is anyone among you suffering? He should pray.
Is anyone happy? He should sing songs of thanks to God.
JAMES 5:13

I have hard days sometimes, Jesus! They don't start out that way. I wake up happy and excited. Then something awful happens, and my mood turns sour. Then things get worse—and my mood gets worse too. (Sorry!) Some days things feel completely unfair! But then I read a verse like this one, and You remind me that even on the bad days I can still have a good attitude. Even on the icky days I can still sing a song of praise to You. No matter what tomorrow looks like—good or bad—I'm going to try to have a happy heart. Amen.

———— THINK ABOUT IT: ————

Who controls your heart?

THANK YOU, JESUS!

I will praise the name of God with song. And I
will give Him great honor with much thanks.
PSALM 69:30

Sometimes I forget to say, "Thanks!" My mom cooks
dinner and does the dishes, and I don't say thank you.
Clean clothes magically appear in my drawers, and I take
it for granted. My dad works hard, and I don't remember
to say, "Thanks for all you do, Dad." My teachers work
hard too, and I forget to say, "Thanks." Sometimes I even
forget to thank *You*, Jesus. Tomorrow, when I wake up,
help me remember all the many, many people I need
to thank for all they've done for me! Amen.

──────── THINK ABOUT IT: ────────

It's fun to have a grateful heart! Is it really
possible to lift someone's spirits just by
offering a smile and a quick "Thank you"?

YOUR KINGDOM COME

"May Your holy nation come. What You want done,
may it be done on earth as it is in heaven."
MATTHEW 6:10

I don't always want what You want, Lord Jesus. I can't
believe I'm admitting that, but it's true. Sometimes I want
things for myself—new toys, new friends, new experi-
ences—but they're not what You want. Sometimes You
withhold the things I want to protect me. (Sometimes
those new friends can lead me down a wrong path!)
Show me how to want what You want—for myself and
for others. Your kingdom come, Your will be done—in
my life and in the lives of those I love. Amen.

——————— **THINK ABOUT IT:** ———————

When is it good to *not* demand your own way
and let God control the situation instead?

I WILL BE BOLD

He kept on preaching about the holy nation
of God. He taught about the Lord Jesus Christ
without fear. No one stopped him.
ACTS 28:31

Sometimes I'm kind of scared to talk to my friends about You, Jesus. Some of them don't believe in You, and they think I'm weird. Others say they believe, but they sure don't act like it. I'm sorry for the times I let them stop me from sharing the good news. Knowing You is the best thing ever, and I want everyone around me to know You too! So please help me be brave. Give me the right words for the right person so I can let them know how great You are. I want to be a good witness, Jesus. . .the very best! Give me courage. Amen.

——————— THINK ABOUT IT: ———————

If you had a miracle cure for cancer, you
would tell everyone, right? The good news of
what Jesus did on the cross is the best news
ever! It's better than the best medicine!

GReat PLaNS!

" 'For I know the plans I have for you,' says the Lord, 'plans for well-being and not for trouble, to give you a future and a hope.' "
JEREMIAH 29:11

Sometimes I wish I could see into the future, Jesus! I don't know where I'm going or how I'm supposed to get there. I must trust that You know all that! You see the things I can't see. You've made plans for my life that I don't understand yet. It's kind of fun—like an adventure—to keep walking ahead even when I don't know where I'm going. But I fully trust You. I know You have good things in store for my life, and that's enough for me!

THINK ABOUT IT:

Has God ever let you down? Hasn't He already proven that His plans for you are good, not bad?

DON'T ACT LIKE THEM

Do not act like the sinful people of the world. Let God change your life. First of all, let Him give you a new mind. Then you will know what God wants you to do. And the things you do will be good and pleasing and perfect.
ROMANS 12:2

Here I am again, Lord Jesus, telling You something You already know. Sometimes I act like the kids I hang out with. . .and not when they're behaving in a good way. Sometimes I let them rub off on me. I don't mean to! I always say I'm going to be a good witness. But then something happens, and I want to fit in, so I go along with what they tell me to do. I always regret it. I always feel so guilty afterward. Please help me start fresh tomorrow. Give me godly friends, and help us all to be more like You. Amen.

—————— THINK ABOUT IT: ——————

Jesus has surrounded you with amazing people who are doing the right things. Does it make sense to only hang out with the ones who are breaking His heart with their behaviors?

THE GOLDEN RULE

"Do to others as you would have them do to you."
LUKE 6:31 NIV

My idea of "do unto others" isn't always the same as Yours, Jesus! Sometimes I want to get even with people who hurt me. I want to embarrass or hurt them (just keeping it real!) because they hurt me. But You want me to live differently. You want me to treat other people the way I *want* to be treated. That changes everything! I want to be treated well. For sure, I want to be included. So I guess that means I must treat others kindly, even when it's hard. Please help me. Amen.

THINK ABOUT IT:

If you really treated people the way you want to be treated, what would change?

YOU OWN IT ALL, JESUS!

And my God will give you everything you need because of His great riches in Christ Jesus.
Philippians 4:19

You own everything, Lord Jesus! You're like the richest person on the planet, but a gazillion times more! Everything I can see with my eyes belongs to You. Sometimes I see my parents worry about money. They wish they had more of it. But I know we can trust You to make sure we have everything we need, because You own it all! Thank You for the promise from Your Word that You share Your riches with Your kids! Amen.

THINK ABOUT IT:

God is your good, good Father. Can you count on Him for everything?

WANTS AND NEEDS

The Lord is my Shepherd. I will have everything I need.
PSALM 23:1

I have a lot of stuff, Lord, but I'm always wanting more, more, more. My friends have a lot of cool stuff, and sometimes I feel a little jealous. But then I remember that You've given me a nice place to live, food on my plate, and clothes to wear. You've also given me people who love me, and that's good enough for me, Lord! Tonight, as I settle into bed, I'm feeling extra grateful for all You've given me today. Thanks for taking such good care of me! Amen.

THINK ABOUT IT:

God promises to give you what you need,
not what you want. Do you have a hard time
figuring out which is which sometimes?

LIVING IN PEACE WITH OTHERS

When the ways of a man are pleasing
to the Lord, He makes even those who
hate him to be at peace with him.
PROVERBS 16:7

Some girls and boys are just hard to be around, Jesus. They're hotheaded and mean. They tell lies. They cheat. They pretend to be good in front of our teachers and other grown-ups, but they're really not who they pretend to be. I know You're watching and You see these people, Lord. They're not easy to get along with. But Your Word promises that if I will have a peaceful attitude, they will simmer down. So I choose to be a peacemaker, Lord. I want to make things better, not worse. Amen.

THINK ABOUT IT:

When someone starts acting angry and
you react with anger, what happens? What
happens if you choose peace instead?

BE A JOY TO HIM

The Lord hates lying lips, but those
who speak the truth are His joy.
PROVERBS 12:22

I don't always tell the truth, Lord Jesus. Sometimes I fib a little. I try to get away with things, so I leave out parts of the story. It's hard to be truthful all the time! Please forgive me for not always being honest. I want to be a joy to You. I know You're saddened when I'm not. Tomorrow is a brand-new day. Help me do my best so that I can bring You happiness through the way I live and the words I speak. Amen.

—————— THINK ABOUT IT: ——————

Would you consider yourself an honest person?
Is there someone in your life you have a hard
time being honest with? Today, you can ask
Jesus to help you bring joy to His heart by always
speaking the truth, even when it's hard.

GUARDING MY WORDS

A poor man who walks with honor is better
than a fool who is sinful in his speaking.
PROVERBS 19:1

My mouth gets me in trouble a lot, Jesus. (You already know this, of course!) Even today I messed up and said some things I shouldn't have. My words weren't always the kindest or the most helpful. I'm so glad You can forgive me for my not-so-great words. Tomorrow I'm going to do my best to speak words that will please Your heart. I want to make You happy, and I want to bless the people I speak to as well. Please help me! Amen.

THINK ABOUT IT:

Your words have power. They're like a
weapon. Do you use them for good or for
evil? Do they cause pleasure or pain?

YOU'RE BIGGER, GOD

God is able to do much more than we ask or think through His power working in us.
EPHESIANS 3:20

You're bigger, Lord God. You're bigger than my problems. You're bigger than that kid who's been bullying me. You're bigger than that math test I'm nervous about. Instead of fretting over how big my problems are, I'm going to start focusing on how much bigger You are. You are a miracle-working God, who is able to do so much more than I can even imagine. Thank You! Amen.

THINK ABOUT IT:

If God created the heavens and the earth, can't He surely take care of the problems you're facing—even the super-big ones?

A PROMISE FROM YOU, GOD

*Respect your father and mother. This is the first Law
given that had a promise. The promise is this: If you
respect your father and mother, you will live a long
time and your life will be full of many good things.*
EPHESIANS 6:2–3

This is an interesting promise, Jesus! If I respect my
parents, I can have a long life filled with good things. It
makes sense, though. The things Mom and Dad tell me
to do are for my own good and for my safety. When they
say, "Don't hang with the wrong friends," it's because
they know that bad friends can lead to trouble. So I'll
stick with Mom and Dad. . .and stick with You, Lord. I'll
respect my parents and the other adults in my life, and
I'll learn to walk in Your ways. Amen.

THINK ABOUT IT:

If you didn't respect your parents, what
would happen? Would you end up going
down a good path or a bad one?

WHO AM I FIGHTING?

*Our fight is not with people. It is against the leaders
and the powers and the spirits of darkness in this world.
It is against the demon world that works in the heavens.*
EPHESIANS 6:12

Sometimes I forget that people aren't my enemy, Jesus.
But the devil certainly is! He causes people to say and
do ugly things, and I lash out at them, forgetting that
he's the one I should be mad at. Tomorrow, as soon as I
wake up, remind me that any battles I face will be against
him, not other people. I won't take it out on my sister.
I won't take it out on my teacher. I won't take it out
on my friends. I'll just let the devil know, once and for
all, that I belong to You and he needs to stop messing
with me! Amen.

THINK ABOUT IT:

When someone says something awful to you,
who put those words in their mouth? Do you
think they came up with those mean words all
on their own, or was the devil behind it?

ALWAYS MEANS ALWAYS!

Always give thanks for all things to God the
Father in the name of our Lord Jesus Christ.
EPHESIANS 5:20

Always means always, Lord. Every single day, every single circumstance, You expect me to give thanks. When I'm happy; when I'm sad. When I'm hurting; when I'm mad. When people have treated me unfairly and unkindly. When I'm making great grades or when I'm failing. No matter what's going on around me, You want the words on my lips to be, "I praise You!" So tonight as I crawl into bed, I say it one last time: the day is done, but my praise goes on, all through the night! Amen.

——————— THINK ABOUT IT: ———————

What makes you feel better—whining and
complaining or having a grateful heart?

I'M GROWING UP!

*When I was a child, I spoke like a child. I thought
like a child. I understood like a child. Now I am
a man. I do not act like a child anymore.*
1 Corinthians 13:11

I've changed a lot over the last few years, Jesus. My face
has changed. My hair has changed. My body has changed.
My clothing choices have changed. Even the things I
like to eat have changed! I'm growing up! When I was
a little kid, I did goofy things; but now that I'm getting
older, I'm doing my best not to be too childish. I want
to be more like You. I've heard that people do most of
their growing while they sleep, so please watch over
me tonight as I grow, grow, grow! Amen.

THINK ABOUT IT:

What if babies never grew up? What if they
never changed? That would be weird, right?
God is always changing you for the better.

A HOPEFUL FUTURE

" 'For I know the plans I have for you,' says
the Lord, 'plans for well-being and not for
trouble, to give you a future and a hope.' "
JEREMIAH 29:11

I love to think about what I'll be like in a few years, Jesus.
It's so crazy to think about what I'll look like. How tall
will I be? How big will my feet be? Will I have the same
friends—or will they be different? What sort of job will I
have one day? I have so much fun imagining. Of course,
You already know the answers to those questions. You
see into my future (cool!), and You know everything. Your
Word says I have a "hopeful" future, so that means You
must have big things ahead for me. I can't wait! Amen.

─── THINK ABOUT IT: ───

Do you trust Jesus with your future? What
are you most excited about? He'll be right
there with you, every step of the way!

BE KIND TO THE UNKIND

"But love those who hate you. Do good to them. Let them use your things and do not expect something back. Your reward will be much. You will be the children of the Most High. He is kind to those who are not thankful and to those who are full of sin."
LUKE 6:35

Okay, I'll admit it—it's a lot easier being kind to those who are kind to me. Even today I struggled to treat some not-so-nice people kindly. But Your Word says I must give kindness away to everyone I meet, no matter how they treat me. Ouch. Tomorrow is a fresh new day, and I know I'll probably run into people who treat me badly. Show me how to bless them with random acts of kindness, Lord, even if I don't feel like it! Amen.

THINK ABOUT IT:

If Jesus was only kind to you when you were behaving well, how often would He be kind to you? Aren't you glad He's kind all the time?

TAKE YOUR MEDICINE!

A glad heart is good medicine, but a
broken spirit dries up the bones.
PROVERBS 17:22

How many times have I heard someone say, "Take your medicine"? If I forget to take my medicine when I'm sick, I won't get well. It's the same thing with joy. Joy is like a medicine for my heart. It makes my heart glad. Sadness makes me feel like I'm sick with the flu. But a little joy goes a long, long way in making me feel better. Tomorrow when I wake up, fill my heart with joy so that I can share it with others who need cheering up. Amen.

THINK ABOUT IT:

Do you know someone who's sad? Maybe God would like you to share some joy with the one who's hurting. In what ways can you share the joy of Jesus?

POWER, LOVE, AND A GOOD MIND

*For God did not give us a spirit of fear. He gave us
a spirit of power and of love and of a good mind.*
2 TIMOTHY 1:7

You don't want me to be afraid, Jesus. Sometimes I forget that. There were a couple of times today when I forgot. But Your Word says that You didn't give me a spirit of fear, so I know those feelings aren't from You. When I get scared, I need to remember that You have given me a different spirit—one of power, love, and a good mind. So I won't panic. I won't flip out and hide, quivering under the covers. I'll face those fears head-on in Jesus' name! Amen.

——————— THINK ABOUT IT: ———————

If fear doesn't come from God, then who—or where—does it come from? You have a very real enemy, and he wants to trip you up. Don't let him!

YOU KNOW MY LIMITS

You have never been tempted to sin in any different way than other people. God is faithful. He will not allow you to be tempted more than you can take. But when you are tempted, He will make a way for you to keep from falling into sin.
1 CORINTHIANS 10:13

You know me so well, Jesus. You know me inside and out. You see how I'm tempted to do things I shouldn't, but You make sure I don't have too much temptation. You always make a way out for me so that I don't end up in trouble. Thanks for looking out for me and for taking such great care of me. I'm so grateful! Amen.

——————— THINK ABOUT IT: ———————

What temptations are hardest for you? Lying? Cheating? Being mean to others? Lashing out in anger? God can take control of that temptation and help you overcome it.

SOMETIMES I FORGET

*But as for you, hold on to what you have learned and
know to be true. Remember where you learned them.*
2 TIMOTHY 3:14

I don't always get it right, Jesus. Sometimes I mess up.
(Oops!) Today I messed up a few times. Tomorrow I
hope to do better. I've learned so much from You, and
I want to do the right things—but sometimes I forget. I
get so busy or so focused on myself that I totally forget
what the Bible says I should do. (Sorry about that!)
Tomorrow I'll do my best to remember Your Word and
then obey! Amen.

THINK ABOUT IT:

How good is your memory? Do you remember
everything you've ever been taught? Of course
not! Some life lessons must be repeated to sink in.
But know that Jesus loves you, no matter what.

THE RIGHT KIND OF FRIENDS

*Do not let anyone fool you. Bad people can make
those who want to live good become bad. Keep
your minds awake! Stop sinning. Some do not
know God at all. I say this to your shame.*
1 CORINTHIANS 15:33–34

I'm not always the best at picking the right friends,
Jesus. Sometimes I spend too much time hanging out
with the kids who don't follow You like they should. I'm
learning that kids who misbehave want me to misbehave
too. They just want me to follow them. But I'm on to
their tricks! I won't do it. I won't let anyone fool me. I'm
keeping my eyes open and my mind alert to their plans.
From now on, I'm picking the right kind of friends. Amen.

THINK ABOUT IT:

There are two kinds of friends—the ones who help
you draw closer to God and the ones who want to
pull you away. Which ones should you hang out with?

YOU DO WHAT YOU SAY, JESUS

*If we tell Him our sins, He is faithful and we
can depend on Him to forgive us of our sins.
He will make our lives clean from all sin.*
1 John 1:9

You don't make promises and then break them, Jesus. I
know a lot of people who do that, but You *never* do. You
say that I can confess my sins (bad deeds) to You, and
You will forgive me, just like that! And You do it every
single time. You're so faithful. I can depend on You to
forgive me, no matter what I've done wrong. Show me
how I can be more dependable like You, Lord. Amen.

———— THINK ABOUT IT: ————

God wants you to tell Him your sins. Do you do
that? . . . Do you confess them to Him? Before
you fall asleep tonight, get those icky things off
your chest. Tell Him. He will forgive you right
away, and you'll have a good night's sleep.

I'M SO ASHAMED SOMETIMES

*Instead of your shame you will have a share
that is twice as much. Instead of being without
honor, they will sing for joy over all you receive.
So they will have twice as much in their land,
and joy that lasts forever will be theirs.*
ISAIAH 61:7

I messed up today, Jesus, and now I'm so embarrassed and ashamed. Everyone knows what I did. I feel so bad in my heart because I know I did the wrong thing. Will these shameful feelings stay with me forever? Please wash them away. When I wake up in the morning, I want to start over again without these icky feelings. Please help me, Jesus. Amen.

THINK ABOUT IT:

Jesus doesn't want you to go on feeling
ashamed once you've asked Him to forgive you.
So why should you let shame hold you back?

HARD WORK

Some good comes from all work.
Nothing but talk leads only to being poor.
PROVERBS 14:23

I work hard some days, Jesus! Other days, I'm pretty lazy. I lie around on the couch or my bed, glad I don't have to go anywhere or do anything. I know You care a lot about hard work. You don't want me to waste too much time. It's good to rest, but too much? . . . That's not healthy. So when I wake up in the morning, give me the energy to get everything done that needs to be done, and all with a smile on my face. Amen.

THINK ABOUT IT:

Why does God care so much about hard work? Is He a hard worker? (Hint: He created the whole world in six days, so. . .)

I WILL GIVE IT TO YOU

*Trust your work to the Lord, and your
plans will work out well.*
PROVERBS 16:3

Sometimes I forget who I'm working for, Jesus. I think
that all my hard work is for me, myself, and I. I set goals,
and I'm excited about reaching them. (Yay!) Then I
remember that all the work I do in this lifetime is really
meant to bring glory to You, not myself. It's all for You.
My plans will work out great as long as I remember that.
So tomorrow I'm going to work hard—not for me, but
for You, Jesus! Amen.

THINK ABOUT IT:

You have big plans and you work hard
to reach those goals. . .but who are you
working for—yourself or Jesus?

CAST IT AWAY

Cast your cares on the LORD and he will sustain you; he will never let the righteous be shaken.
PSALM 55:22 NIV

I know what it means to cast something, Jesus. It's like when you're fishing and you cast the line into the water, far away from yourself. That's what You want me to do with my cares (my troubles). You don't want me to hang on to them. I'm supposed to let go. Today I forgot to let go of some of my troubles, but I'm doing that right now! I'm casting them into the sea of forgetfulness and starting over fresh tomorrow! Amen.

THINK ABOUT IT:

Have you ever been fishing? Have you ever cast your line into the water? Why do you suppose God uses this same idea when He talks about getting rid of your burdens?

LITTLE TONGUE, BIG PROBLEM

*The tongue is also a small part of the body,
but it can speak big things. See how a very
small fire can set many trees on fire.*
JAMES 3:5

My tongue gets me in trouble a lot, Jesus. (I know You know this. You see and hear everything.) I don't mean to smart off to my dad. I don't mean to say ugly things to my brother. I don't mean to be rude to anyone. . .but sometimes I mess up and do it anyway. You say that the tongue is small but fierce! It can set things on fire. I've seen that a time or two. I've started a few fiery troubles with the words from my mouth. Please forgive me and help me start over. Amen.

THINK ABOUT IT:

Why do you suppose God compares the
tongue to a spark that causes a forest fire?

IRON SHARPENS IRON

*Iron is made sharp with iron, and one
man is made sharp by a friend.*
PROVERBS 27:17

I'm starting to get it, Jesus! We become more like the people we hang out with. When I hang out with not-so-great people, they rub off on me. When I hang out with people who love You, I become more like them. I get "sharper" in my faith when I spend time with them. Please show me the very best people I should be hanging out with. I want to be a good witness to everyone, but I want to learn from the very best!

—————— THINK ABOUT IT: ——————

How does spending time with faith-filled
people help you grow in your faith?

BEFORE THE DAY IS DONE

If you are angry, do not let it become sin.
Get over your anger before the day is finished.
EPHESIANS 4:26

Temper, temper! Some days I have a terrible temper, Lord. I get to the end of the day, and I'm ready to crawl into bed, but I'm still mad about something that happened hours before. Your Word says this should not be so! I shouldn't go to bed angry. I need to get rid of that anger before it becomes sin. So right here and right now, I ask You to forgive me for my temper. I give it all to You so I can have a good night's sleep and wake up in a great mood. Amen.

THINK ABOUT IT:

Why does Jesus want you to get rid of anger
before you get into bed? Why does it matter?

I'M ASKING, JESUS!

If you do not have wisdom, ask God for it.
He is always ready to give it to you and will
never say you are wrong for asking.
JAMES 1:5

It feels like I'm always asking for stuff, Jesus. At Christmas my list is pretty long. For my birthday? Yeah, I have a list then too! I'm always asking my parents or grandparents for stuff. Sometimes I forget that I can come to You to ask for the important things. . .like wisdom. When I ask, You're quick to give me what I need. And I'm learning that what I want and what I need are two different things. Thank You for loving me enough to give me the important stuff. Amen.

THINK ABOUT IT:

Would you consider yourself needy? Are you always asking for stuff? Who do you bug the most? Why not take those requests to God instead?

LISTEN MUCH, SPEAK LITTLE

*My Christian brothers, you know everyone
should listen much and speak little.
He should be slow to become angry.*
JAMES 1:19

Uh-oh! This is a tough one, Jesus. I don't always listen. I'm usually too busy trying to get my point across. I want people to understand how I feel. But sometimes it's better if I keep my lips closed and my ears open. Other people have important things to say too. I don't want to miss anything because I'm so busy blabbering on. I need Your help, Lord! Amen.

THINK ABOUT IT:

God gave you two ears and only one mouth.
Why do you suppose that is? Could it be that
He wants you to listen more and speak less?

I WILL KEEP RUNNING

All these many people who have had faith in God are around us like a cloud. Let us put every thing out of our lives that keeps us from doing what we should. Let us keep running in the race that God has planned for us.
HEBREWS 12:1

I get so tired sometimes, Jesus! I'm always on the go! School. Friends. Family stuff. Church. Sports. It's a lot! There are nights when I climb into bed so exhausted I wonder if I can keep going. But You tell me I can. . .and I should! So I'll keep running the race, no matter how hard it might seem. I want to be like the great men and women of the Bible who ran their race all the way to the very end! Amen.

THINK ABOUT IT:

What if Noah hadn't built the ark? What if Moses hadn't led the Israelites to the Promised Land?

ME, MYSELF, AND PRIDE

*Pride comes before being destroyed and
a proud spirit comes before a fall.*
PROVERBS 16:18

I get a little prideful sometimes, Jesus. I like to brag on myself. When I accomplish something great—like earning a good grade on my report card or getting a good score in a sporting competition—I tell everyone about it. I get a little puffed up as I brag, brag, brag. You tell me to be careful, not to let my pride get too big! People who make a big deal out of how great they think they are usually end up looking foolish in the end. So please help me to watch my pride, Lord! Amen.

—————— THINK ABOUT IT: ——————

Are there any feelings of pride you need
to get rid of? Ask God for help. Make
tomorrow about others, not yourself.

HAPPY WITH WHAT I HAVE

Keep your lives free from the love of money.
Be happy with what you have. God has said,
"I will never leave you or let you be alone." So
we can say for sure, "The Lord is my Helper. I am
not afraid of anything man can do to me."
HEBREWS 13:5–6

I want. . .a lot. I'm always asking for stuff, Jesus. New stuff, cool stuff. . .lots of stuff. It's not that I need all that stuff. I'm just never really satisfied with all I have. But Your Word says I should be satisfied. I'm not supposed to be in love with money or the stuff it can buy. I know that You've got me covered. I'll never want for anything. So please help me put away the desire to have more, more, more. What I have is plenty! (And did I mention how grateful I am for all You've given me?) Thanks so much, Jesus! Amen.

THINK ABOUT IT:

The things you want. . .are they critical? Can you live without them? Are there better ways that money could be spent? Just something to think about!

I'M NOT LIKE EVERYONE ELSE

We all have different gifts that God has given to us by His loving-favor. We are to use them. If someone has the gift of preaching the Good News, he should preach. He should use the faith God has given him.
ROMANS 12:6

I'm not like everyone else, Jesus, and that's okay! I don't want to be a cookie-cutter copy, after all! It's all right with me that I'm different. You gave me different dreams, different gifts, different opinions, even different looks! I'm unique. You planned it that way on purpose. (The world would be pretty boring if everyone looked the same and had the same talents.) Thanks for making me unique. I promise to be the best me I can be! Amen.

———— THINK ABOUT IT: ————

Why do you suppose God made everyone unique? Why don't all human beings look the same? God is very creative, isn't He?

WHAT WILL I BE?

Christ gave gifts to men. He gave to some the gift to be missionaries, some to be preachers, others to be preachers who go from town to town. He gave others the gift to be church leaders and teachers. These gifts help His people work well for Him.
EPHESIANS 4:11–12

It's fun to think about what I'll be when I grow up, Lord Jesus. Will I be a teacher? A dad? An astronaut? Will I work on computers? Own a farm? Play sports? I have all sorts of dreams, but it's really up to You. For sure, You have placed gifts inside of me, and I know You will use them, no matter my age. These gifts are meant to bless the world—whether I'm young or old. Thanks for Your great gifts! Amen.

―――――――― **THINK ABOUT IT**: ――――――――

Does God know what you're going
to be when you grow up?

THINGS DON'T BRING LIFE

Then Jesus said to them all, "Watch yourselves!
Keep from wanting all kinds of things you
should not have. A man's life is not made up
of things, even if he has many riches."
LUKE 12:15

I look around my bedroom and I see lots of things, Jesus. I see my bed, my covers, even the pajamas I'm wearing! I see a dresser with clothes in the drawers. I see a closet with stuff jammed inside. I see my shoes and my other belongings. I'm surrounded by stuff! But You have reminded me with this verse that "stuff" isn't what makes life great. Loving You and loving people (my family and friends) is really where I find life. Amen.

———— THINK ABOUT IT: ————

Why did Jesus remind us that life isn't made up of stuff? After all, we have a lot of it! What do you think He's trying to teach us?

NO FAVORITES!

My Christian brothers, our Lord Jesus Christ is the Lord of shining-greatness. Since your trust is in Him, do not look on one person as more important than another.
JAMES 2:1

Sometimes I play favorites. I don't realize I'm doing it until someone else points it out. But I'll hang out with one friend and ignore the others. Or I'll spend time with one sister but not the other. It's easy to do, Jesus! I'm naturally drawn to some people. But I'm glad You remind me that I need to work harder to include others so they don't feel "less than." You never make me feel "less than," and I don't want to make others feel that way either. Thanks for reminding me. Amen.

THINK ABOUT IT:

Have you ever been in a situation where someone left you out? How did it make you feel?

I WILL FORGIVE

*When you stand to pray, if you have anything
against anyone, forgive him. Then your Father
in heaven will forgive your sins also.*
MARK 11:25

I'm not always quick to forgive others, Jesus. Sometimes I get hurt and hold on to the pain for hours or even days. I have a hard time letting go. But Your Word says that I should forgive others so that You will forgive me. I don't want anything to get in the way of my relationship with You, so tonight, before I go to sleep, I'm going to do my best to forgive the ones who have hurt me—even if they never asked for my forgiveness. It's the right thing to do. Amen.

———— THINK ABOUT IT: ————

When you don't forgive someone who has
hurt you, what are the consequences?

HOW MANY TIMES?

Then Peter came to Jesus and said, "Lord, how many times may my brother sin against me and I forgive him, up to seven times?" Jesus said to him, "I tell you, not seven times but seventy times seven!"
MATTHEW 18:21–22

It's not enough for me to forgive someone once, is it, Jesus? The Bible says I have to forgive over and over and over again. This isn't easy! (I guess You already know that.) Some people are mean to me. . .a lot. So I need to forgive a lot. I'll go on forgiving and trust You to work inside the mean person's heart. Just because I forgive doesn't mean I have to be close friends with them, after all. Thanks for forgiving me over and over, by the way. Amen.

THINK ABOUT IT:

It might seem like a lot for God to expect you to forgive someone more than once, but how many times has He forgiven you?

I WILL WATCH MY TALK

Watch your talk! No bad words should be coming from your mouth. Say what is good. Your words should help others grow as Christians.
EPHESIANS 4:29

I wonder what it would be like to read back over all my words at the end of the day, Lord. Even now I'm thinking of some of the things I said today. Those words wouldn't make a very good book. Some words were goofy. Some were angry. Some were brimming with frustration. I didn't always bring honor to You with the things that came out of my mouth. Tomorrow I will watch my talk. I'll try to keep bad stuff from coming out of my mouth. I'll only say what's good so that I can honor You. Amen.

———— THINK ABOUT IT: ————

If you never guarded your words, what would happen over time? Would the quality of your words get better or worse with time?

I WON'T JUDGE

*Do not say what is wrong in other people's lives.
Then other people will not say what is wrong in
your life. Do not say someone is guilty. Then other
people will not say you are guilty. Forgive other
people and other people will forgive you.*
LUKE 6:37

I get a little bit judgy at times, Lord. I see the mistakes that others make, and I want to correct them. But You say it's not my place to try to fix the mess-ups my friends and family members make. You will help them do better next time. If I'm too quick to point out every little flaw, they will probably start judging me too. And that doesn't feel good. Instead, I'll just forgive and pray for the person and leave the outcome up to You. Amen.

THINK ABOUT IT:

Why is God the only one who should
judge people? Is it because He's the only
one who can see into their hearts?

YOU'VE LOVED ME A LONG TIME

Even before the world was made, God chose us for Himself because of His love. He planned that we should be holy and without blame as He sees us.
EPHESIANS 1:4

This scripture verse is so cool, Jesus! You knew who I was even before the world was created. How is that even possible? I wasn't born yet! I didn't have a name. I had no hair or eyes or freckles. And yet, somehow, You knew and loved me? That tells me You always had a plan for my life, even before my mother became my mother. My heart feels happy when I realize You've always known me best of all. Amen.

———— THINK ABOUT IT: ————

How long have you known your family members? How long have you known your friends? Jesus has known you much, much longer than that!

YOUR POWER IS IN ME

I pray that you will know how great His power is for those who have put their trust in Him. It is the same power that raised Christ from the dead. This same power put Christ at God's right side in heaven.
EPHESIANS 1:19–20

Some days I feel like such a weakling. I don't have the energy to tackle my problems or my chores. I just feel. . .blah. Then I am reminded of this verse. You say that the same power that raised Jesus from the dead lives inside of me. Whoa! That's a lot of power! You've given it to me as a gift but also so that I can lead others to You. Help me as I share the good news of what You've done in my life. Thank You for Your power! Amen.

——— THINK ABOUT IT: ———

If the same power that raised Jesus from the dead lives in you, what are you waiting for? Get over that fear and get busy telling others about Him!

THE BEST GUIDE

*For the Lord will be your trust. He will
keep your foot from being caught.*
PROVERBS 3:26

If I went on a long walk in a national park, I would want a really good guide, someone who knew the way. A guide would know where the dangers were—steep holes in the path, bears in the woods, broken tree branches, and so on. With a guide leading the way, I would be very safe. That's what You are, Jesus. You're the best guide ever. You lay out my path and I take safe steps, knowing You're right there with me, leading the way. You will keep my foot from being caught in a trap! Thanks for always guiding me. Amen.

THINK ABOUT IT:

If you headed out into the woods completely alone, would you feel safe? Why is having a guide so helpful?

I WON'T GIVE UP

Do not let yourselves get tired of doing good. If we do not give up, we will get what is coming to us at the right time.
GALATIANS 6:9

Sometimes I do the right thing but it doesn't work out. I'm nice to someone who's been ugly to me. Or I decide not to cheat on a test even after the boy next to me in class tells me I should. But then things don't always end up right. The teacher still thinks I'm the one who's cheating. The mean kid spreads ugly rumors about me. Still, I won't give up, Jesus. You say I should never get tired of doing the right thing. . .and I won't! Amen.

THINK ABOUT IT:

Jesus always did the right thing, but He still faced troubles. What can you learn from His story?

YOUR PEACE IS GREATER

The peace of God is much greater than the human mind can understand. This peace will keep your hearts and minds through Christ Jesus.
PHILIPPIANS 4:7

There's not a lot of peace in my heart some days, Lord. I get upset with people and it's hard to let go of what I'm feeling. My heart feels like it's twisted up and my thoughts are crazy. But I know You can bring peace, even in the middle of the storm going on inside of me. Thank You for calming things down. I could never do that on my own. Amen.

THINK ABOUT IT:

If a storm never calmed, what would eventually happen? Would the same be true for a storm inside of you?

YOU ARE A FATHER WHO HELPS

As a father helps his children, you know how we
wanted to help you and give you comfort. We told
you with strong words that you should live to please
God. He is the One Who chose you to come into His
holy nation and to share His shining-greatness.
1 Thessalonians 2:11–12

You're the very best kind of Father, Lord God. You're teaching me lessons every minute of every day. (There's so much to learn!) You help me when I'm in trouble too. I never have to wonder if You're going to rush to my side to pull me out of a mess or walk with me right through it. You do it every time. Thank You for helping me! Amen.

———— THINK ABOUT IT: ————

How weird would it be to have a father who
never helped you with anything? Maybe he never
fed you as a baby. Never taught you to tie your
shoes. Didn't show you how to eat with a fork
or spoon. What kind of father would that be?

I WON'T SHAKE WITH FEAR

"Be strong and have strength of heart. Do not be afraid or shake with fear because of them. For the Lord your God is the One Who goes with you. He will be faithful to you. He will not leave you alone."
DEUTERONOMY 31:6

It doesn't feel cool to admit it, but I get scared sometimes, Lord. People think boys are supposed to be brave all the time. But honestly? I'm not. I let fear rise up in my heart sometimes. I guess that's normal, right? Thanks for the reminder that You will take my fears. You're always close by, ready to calm me down when I'm scared. I'm so grateful. Amen.

--------- THINK ABOUT IT: ---------

Why do you suppose boys have a hard time admitting when they're afraid? Can you take all your fears to God?

I WON'T GO BY WHAT I SEE

*Our life is lived by faith. We do not live
by what we see in front of us.*
2 CORINTHIANS 5:7

Are my eyes deceiving me, Lord? I feel like a mountain is looming in front of me! My problems are so big, they seem impossible to overcome. You tell me I can live by faith, not by sight. I'm counting on that right now, because my eyes are trying to convince me that the problem is way too big. I'll rest easy, though, because I know that nothing is too big for You. Thanks for handling my problems! Amen.

———— THINK ABOUT IT: ————

How many times have you been worried
about a problem? Did God take care of those
problems in the past? Do you think He'll take
care of any problem you face in the future?

I WILL RUN THE RACE

All these many people who have had faith in God are around us like a cloud. Let us put every thing out of our lives that keeps us from doing what we should. Let us keep running in the race that God has planned for us.
HEBREWS 12:1

I love to run, Lord God! Races are a blast. I love that feeling I get when the caller yells, "Ready, set. . .go!" I take off like a horse out of the gate! At first I'm really, really fast. But then I start to get tired. I slow down. My legs feel wobbly. I wonder if I'll make it to the finish line. Thanks for reminding me that You want me to keep going. I won't stop! Amen.

———— THINK ABOUT IT: ————

If an Olympic runner stopped before reaching the finish line, would he get the prize?

YOU'RE MY SAFE PLACE

God is our safe place and our strength. He is always our help when we are in trouble. So we will not be afraid, even if the earth is shaken and the mountains fall into the center of the sea, and even if its waters go wild with storm and the mountains shake with its action.
PSALM 46:1–3

When I play baseball, I'm always trying to make it around all of the bases to home plate. Home plate is my safe place. When I'm there, nothing can hurt me. You are the real safe place, Jesus. When I run to You, absolutely nothing can touch me. You protect me and keep me safe. Thanks for being my "home plate"! Amen.

THINK ABOUT IT:

What if a baseball field had no home plate? What would happen?

BECAUSE YOU LOVE

*For God so loved the world that He gave His only
Son. Whoever puts his trust in God's Son will not
be lost but will have life that lasts forever.*
JOHN 3:16

You love. . .and so You give, Lord. You gave Your only
Son to die on the cross for me, to forgive me of my
sins. Now You're showing me how to love others. Loving
means giving, so I will do my best to give as You gave. I
will give joy. I will give kindness. I will give gentleness.
When people ask, "Why are you treating me so well?" I'll
say, "I learned from Jesus, the very best teacher!" Amen.

——————— **THINK ABOUT IT:** ———————

Why are loving people so giving?

I WILL STAY AWAKE

Watch and keep awake! Stand true to the Lord. Keep on acting like men and be strong. Everything you do should be done in love.
1 CORINTHIANS 16:13–14

Sometimes I hear a TV show playing and the language is bad. I just ignore it and keep watching. Or I'll be hanging out with a friend who uses inappropriate language...but I don't leave. It's almost like I've fallen asleep at the wheel and don't notice when inappropriate things happen anymore. You want me to stay wide awake, Lord God. It's important to You that I keep watching and responding appropriately. Help me to be strong. I want to walk away from inappropriate things, but I'll need Your help for sure. Amen.

THINK ABOUT IT:

What if no one ever took a stand for what's right?

I WON'T BE LIKE THEM

Do not act like the sinful people of the world.
Let God change your life. First of all, let Him
give you a new mind. Then you will know what
God wants you to do. And the things you do
will be good and pleasing and perfect.
ROMANS 12:2

This is a hard one, Lord. I want to be accepted and part of the group—at school, in the neighborhood, and at church. But sometimes the other kids do or say things that are not okay. Your Word tells me not to be like those kids. I must keep standing for You. So I ask for Your courage to be different, even when it's really, really hard. The world will only know what You're like if someone like me takes a stand for truth. Amen.

———— THINK ABOUT IT: ————

God wants your behavior to be good, pleasing,
and perfect. How can that happen?

I WILL DO WHAT MY PARENTS SAY

Hear your father's teaching, my son, and do not turn away from your mother's teaching. For they are a glory to your head and a chain of beauty around your neck.
PROVERBS 1:8–9

Here's a confession, Lord: I don't always do what my parents say. I know You know this already. You see and hear everything. It breaks Your heart—and theirs—when I do my own thing, but sometimes it's so hard to obey! Thank You for this verse. It reminds me that obedience matters to You. So I'll listen. I'll obey. The things Mom and Dad are asking me to do are for my own good, after all! Amen.

──── THINK ABOUT IT: ────

What if toddlers never listened to or obeyed their parents? How would they learn the really important things—like not running out into the street or playing with matches?

I WILL THINK ABOUT IT

Christian brothers, keep your minds thinking about whatever is true, whatever is respected, whatever is right, whatever is pure, whatever can be loved, and whatever is well thought of. If there is anything good and worth giving thanks for, think about these things.
PHILIPPIANS 4:8

Sometimes my mind wanders, Lord. I'm in the middle of history class and my teacher is going on and on, and I check out. My mind goes to a different place. I start thinking about how angry I am with my friend for what he said. I think up ways to keep from obeying my parents. My thoughts get kind of messed up. You want me to stay focused on things that matter—on good and perfect things. I need Your help with this, Jesus! Amen.

———— THINK ABOUT IT: ————

What are some ways you can keep your brain focused on things that are right and good?

BEING YOUNG IS COOL!

Let no one show little respect for you because you are young. Show other Christians how to live by your life. They should be able to follow you in the way you talk and in what you do. Show them how to live in faith and in love and in holy living.
1 TIMOTHY 4:12

Some people look down on me because I'm younger than they are. That stinks! I don't like to feel "less than" others, Lord. But Your Word reminds me that I'm *not* less than! You say that no one should look down on those who are younger. I guess that means I can't look down on the kids younger than me, either. Help me with this, please. Amen.

THINK ABOUT IT:

There will always be older and younger people. What would happen if we all treated each other kindly?

WHO AM I TRYING TO PLEASE?

*Do you think I am trying to get the favor of men,
or of God? If I were still trying to please men,
I would not be a servant owned by Christ.*
GALATIANS 1:10

Sometimes I'm a people-pleaser, Lord. I want everyone to like me, and so I do stuff hoping to impress them. I don't let them see my struggles because I want them to think I'm cool. But You say I shouldn't try to please people. What matters is that I please You. It's Your favor that's most important, and You don't want me to hide my mess-ups. You love me no matter what! Thanks for the reminder that You love me even when I make mistakes. Amen.

―――――――――― **THINK ABOUT IT:** ――――――――――

It's good to have friends, but what would happen if you spent all your time trying to impress others?

WITH ALL I AM

The man said, "You must love the Lord your God with all your heart. You must love Him with all your soul. You must love Him with all your strength. You must love Him with all your mind. You must love your neighbor as you love yourself."
LUKE 10:27

The Bible says I'm supposed to love You with everything I am. . .my heart, my strength, my mind. . .my *everything!* Sometimes (just keeping it real) I put other things first— my stuff, my relationships, my hopes and dreams. Then I remember that Your Word says I should always give You first place, Lord. Tomorrow when I wake up, I plan to do just that, but I will definitely need You with me every step of the way. Amen.

———— THINK ABOUT IT: ————

Why do you suppose God wants
to be first in your life?

IF I PUT YOU FIRST. . .

"First of all, look for the holy nation of God. Be right with Him. All these other things will be given to you also."
MATTHEW 6:33

If I put You first, Jesus, then everything else falls into place. You make sure I have every single thing I need—food to eat, clothes to wear, a roof over my head. . .all of it! If I need it, You're going to provide it, as long as I remember You come first—above it all. I won't let anything else in my life become too important. I'll remember it's all about You, Jesus. Amen.

--- **THINK ABOUT IT**: ---

Why is God the best boss ever? What happens when you listen to Him?

ARMED FOR BATTLE

Put on the things God gives you to fight with. Then you will not fall into the traps of the devil. Our fight is not with people. It is against the leaders and the powers and the spirits of darkness in this world. It is against the demon world that works in the heavens.
EPHESIANS 6:11–12

I can't imagine going onto the battlefield without the right weapons or armor, Lord. I would lose the battle very quickly if I wasn't prepared. The same is true with the spiritual battles I face. The enemy is out to get me, and I have to be prepared to fight him. I will wear Your armor to stay safe. Thank You for reminding me that people aren't my enemy. I won't fight them. I will fight the devil, and I will win in Jesus' name! Amen.

THINK ABOUT IT:

Does it change your thinking to know that people are not the real enemy—that Satan is the one who's trying to take you down?

FOLLOW THE RIGHT LEADER

"Follow the Lord your God and fear Him.
Keep His Laws, and listen to His voice.
Work for Him, and hold on to Him."
DEUTERONOMY 13:4

I remember playing Follow the Leader when I was a kid, Lord. I always wanted to be the leader, the one telling everyone else where to go. In real life I want to be a good leader, one who leads others to You. I don't want to follow behind those who break Your heart with their actions. They will lead me down the wrong path for sure! Instead, help me stay focused on the prize as I boldly follow You. Amen.

THINK ABOUT IT:

Have you ever been guilty of following after
the wrong crowd? If you pick the wrong
leader to follow, what could go wrong?

FOCUS, KID! FOCUS!

Let your eyes look straight in front of you,
and keep looking at what is in front of you.
PROVERBS 4:25

Lord God, I know I'm supposed to be paying attention to my teacher or my parents, but it's so hard! I get distracted and begin to think about a problem I'm going through or a fight I had with my friend—and I quit listening. This happens a lot in class and even at church sometimes. From now on, help me stay focused on the things that matter to You. Amen.

THINK ABOUT IT:

How can you stay better focused when your parents or teachers are talking?

WHEN I MESS UP

My dear children, I am writing this to you so you will not sin. But if anyone does sin, there is One Who will go between him and the Father. He is Jesus Christ, the One Who is right with God.
1 JOHN 2:1

I'm not perfect, Lord. You've definitely figured that out already! I make *a lot* of mistakes. Sometimes I end up feeling really guilty for the bad things I've done. But the Bible reminds me that when I mess up, You create a way for me to make things right again. You sent Your Son, Jesus, to take my sin and shame. Thank You for loving me so much, Father God. Amen.

—— THINK ABOUT IT: ——

If Jesus hadn't died on the cross and taken your sins, how would you ever get to heaven?

IT'S NOT MY BODY

*Do you not know that your body is a house
of God where the Holy Spirit lives? God
gave you His Holy Spirit. Now you belong to
God. You do not belong to yourselves.*
1 CORINTHIANS 6:19

My body belongs to You, Lord—every part of it, from
my head to my toes. And how I treat my body matters.
That's why I do my best not to eat too much junk food
or stay up too late. I want to take care of myself because
Your Spirit lives inside of me. I don't want Your Spirit to
have to live in a broken-down house or a house that's
exhausted and overloaded with sugar. I want to give
You my very best, Lord. Amen.

———— THINK ABOUT IT: ————

If you didn't take care of your body,
what would happen over time?

IT'S ALL GOING TO WORK OUT

*We know that God makes all things work
together for the good of those who love Him
and are chosen to be a part of His plan.*
ROMANS 8:28

You have a way of working everything out, Lord God.
Even when things look basically impossible to me, You
always come through. You're a wonder-working God!
And all that bad stuff I go through. . .You even use that
for good in my life. I won't get upset when hard times
come, because I know You're going to turn the hard
stuff around and use it in an amazing way. You've done
it time and time again, and I'm so grateful! Amen.

——————— **THINK ABOUT IT:** ———————

How can God make something good
from a very bad situation?

I WILL ASK

"Ask, and what you are asking for will be given to you. Look, and what you are looking for you will find. Knock, and the door you are knocking on will be opened to you."
MATTHEW 7:7

Sometimes I forget that I can ask You for stuff, Lord. Like peace when I'm going through a hard time. Or joy when I'm feeling really upset or angry. Or kindness when I don't feel like being kind to the person who hurt me. I can (literally!) ask You for anything, and You will hear and answer. So today I'm asking. I'm looking. I'm knocking. And I know You won't let me down. You never have—not even once! Thanks, Father God! Amen.

THINK ABOUT IT:

What area of your life are you struggling in the most today? Will you let Jesus take control of that area for you?

I WON'T LOVE STUFF

*Do not love the world or anything
in the world. If anyone loves the world,
the Father's love is not in him.*
1 JOHN 2:15

When I look around me as I climb into bed at night, I see lots and lots of stuff, Lord. My room is packed full! I've got electronics, clothes, toys, sports equipment, books. . .so much stuff! Sometimes it's tempting to love my stuff and want more of it (especially electronics and sports stuff). I crave more and more. But Your Word says I shouldn't love stuff. It shouldn't be the most important thing to me. So please teach me how to say no to stuff. I've got plenty already! Amen.

THINK ABOUT IT:

How are wants and needs different?

KINDNESS MATTERS

You must be kind to each other. Think of the other person. Forgive other people just as God forgave you because of Christ's death on the cross.
EPHESIANS 4:32

Some people are easier to be kind to than others, Lord God. You see how it is! There are boys (and even some girls) who are so mean that I have a hard time not reacting in anger. I want to get really, really mad at them. It doesn't make a lot of sense to me that I'm supposed to treat the mean ones with kindness, but I'm willing to try it Your way. Tomorrow when I wake up, give me the courage to be kind—even to the really mean kids. I'm definitely going to need Your help! Amen.

THINK ABOUT IT:

Is Jesus always kind to you, even when you don't deserve it?

THESE LIPS WON'T LIE

A faithful man who tells what he knows will not lie, but the man who is not faithful will lie.
PROVERBS 14:5

I can't say I've always been honest. You know the truth, Lord. Some days I mess up big time. I don't mean to do it, but little white lies slide right out of my mouth. Then sometimes they become even bigger lies as I attempt to cover them up. What a fiasco! Your Word is very clear: You don't want me to lie. So I'm going to do my best from now on to speak only the truth, even when it's really, really hard. I'll need courage, but You're good at supplying that. Thanks for helping me with this. Amen.

———— THINK ABOUT IT: ————

Why does God feel so strongly about His kids speaking only the truth? Why does it matter to Him? Could it be because You represent Him to others?

ALWAYS FULL OF JOY

*Be full of joy always because you belong to
the Lord. Again I say, be full of joy!*
PHILIPPIANS 4:4

Some days I don't feel very joyful. I'm sad. I'm upset. I'm
angry. I'm worried. I'm anything but joyful. Is it possible,
even in the middle of a really bad day, to have joy? Your
Word says I need to try, so I will. Remind me, when I'm
in the middle of a rough time, to ask You to fill my joy
tank. I know that laughter is good, like medicine. It helps
take away the pain. So come and fill me up, I pray. Amen.

——————— THINK ABOUT IT: ———————

If you were having a terrible day but then someone
made you laugh, would you feel better?

YOU MADE ME

For You made the parts inside me. You put me together inside my mother. I will give thanks to You, for the greatness of the way I was made brings fear. Your works are great and my soul knows it very well.
PSALM 139:13–14

It's weird to think that You know what I look like, not just on the outside, but on the inside too, Lord God. You know what my bones look like. And my muscles. And my tendons. You know every beat of my heart. You literally see it all and know it all, because You created me! I'm different from everyone else I know. . .and that's okay. I don't need to look like them. You made me exactly as I am, and You love me no matter what. Thank You! Amen.

THINK ABOUT IT:

Why didn't God make all of us to look alike? Why do we have different hair colors, eye colors, skin colors, and so on?

THINKING ABOUT HEAVEN

Keep your minds thinking about things in heaven.
Do not think about things on the earth.
COLOSSIANS 3:2

I get so worked up about earthly stuff sometimes—like getting my own way. Like winning every argument. Like making sure everyone likes me. I let myself get jealous of others, and I even let my temper loose sometimes. Whenever those things happen, I realize that I'm more focused on the things of this earth than the things of heaven. Help me get past the earthly things to think about the things that really matter to You. Amen.

THINK ABOUT IT:

In heaven there's no anger. There are no lies. There are no arguments or fights. There's no jealousy. What will that be like?

BEFORE I WAS BORN

*"Before I started to put you together in your mother,
I knew you. Before you were born, I set you apart as
holy. I chose you to speak to the nations for Me."*
JEREMIAH 1:5

It's crazy cool to think that You knew me before I was born, Lord God. I wasn't even here yet. . .and You already knew everything about me. You knew what color my eyes would be, what my hair and skin would look like. You knew if I would be hyper or quiet, someone who loves to study or someone who's not happy in school. You literally knew it all. And You had a special plan for my life even then! I'm so glad You know and love me, Father God! Amen.

THINK ABOUT IT:

The same God who created you knows
everything about you. Do you think you can
trust Him to fix the broken areas of your life?

NO WHINING OR COMPLAINING

Be glad you can do the things you should be doing.
Do all things without arguing and talking about
how you wish you did not have to do them.
PHILIPPIANS 2:14

This is a hard one, Lord! Sometimes I like to whine and complain, especially when my parents are making me do something I really don't want to do. I figure if I pitch a big enough fit, they'll eventually change their minds. That hardly ever happens, though. I've tried that same trick with my teachers before, and they didn't like it either. Your Word says I shouldn't grumble about stuff I don't want to do. I should just obey with a joyful heart. I'm definitely going to need Your help with this! Amen.

──────── THINK ABOUT IT: ────────

If you had to add up all the hours that you've spent whining and complaining in your life, how many hours would it come to?

I WILL WORK FOR YOU

We are His work. He has made us to belong
to Christ Jesus so we can work for Him.
He planned that we should do this.
EPHESIANS 2:10

You created us because You wanted companionship with us, didn't You, Lord? I know You love us. But You also created us to share the good news with others. You've given each of us special gifts so we can let others know about You in the best possible way. Some people are singers. Some are writers. Some are good with computers and electronics. All of these gifts can be used to share the story of why You came, Jesus, and how You save us because You love us. Thanks for using me! Amen.

———— THINK ABOUT IT: ————

The things you're good at, the things
you love to do. . .aren't they all special
gifts God picked just for you?

WHO'S IN CHARGE?

Do not let sin have power over you.
Let good have power over sin!
ROMANS 12:21

Sometimes I feel like I have no power at all, Lord. I feel like a real weakling. Then I read the Bible and see verses like this one and realize I have control over sin in my life. I can choose not to give in to temptation. I can overcome it with Your help. So today I want to remind the enemy, "You have no power here!" Through the power of the Spirit, I am an overcomer. In Jesus' name, I have all the power I need. Amen!

THINK ABOUT IT:

Would Jesus ever leave you powerless
to face the enemy alone?

I WANT TO MAKE YOU HAPPY

Children, obey your parents in everything.
The Lord is pleased when you do.
COLOSSIANS 3:20

I'm always looking for ways to be happy. Sometimes I do that by asking my parents for more stuff. But I'm learning that stuff won't make me happy. When I finally learn to do the things my parents and the other adults in my life ask me to do, my obedience makes Your heart happy, Lord. And making You happy is the very best thing of all. So when I wake up tomorrow, help me remember that making You happy is what makes me happy! Instead of putting myself first, I'll obey and put You first. Amen.

———— THINK ABOUT IT: ————

Why do you suppose God is happy when you obey your parents? Why would He care?

I WON'T BE ME-FOCUSED

Do not always be thinking about your own plans only.
Be happy to know what other people are doing.
PHILIPPIANS 2:4

I want to do what I want to do. I want to go where I want to go. I guess it's obvious I'm too me-focused sometimes, Jesus. It's hard to remember that what others need is just as important as what I want. Help me turn my focus to them. Get rid of the selfishness in me, please. Becoming others-focused won't be easy, but with Your help I know it can be done! Show me how to care as much about others as I do myself. Amen.

THINK ABOUT IT:

What would the world be like if people only cared about themselves? How would babies and sick people survive?

THE WAY I LOVE MYSELF

"The second is like it, 'You must love your neighbor as you love yourself.'"
MATTHEW 22:39

What does it look like to love others as I love myself, Lord? Does it mean I have to consider their feelings as important as my own? Does it mean I put their comfort and safety alongside my own? Your Word tells me that loving them "as I love myself" is important to You. I confess, I love myself a lot. I usually put myself first. But I'll do it Your way, Jesus. I'll start loving others the way I love me. Amen.

―――――――――― **THINK ABOUT IT:** ――――――――――

What does love look like? How does it
act? Why does it matter to Jesus?

I WON'T SHOW OFF

*Nothing should be done because of pride
or thinking about yourself. Think of other
people as more important than yourself.*
PHILIPPIANS 2:3

Okay, I'll admit it, Lord. . .sometimes I do stuff just to show off. I like to make people look my way so they can say, "Wow, you're really talented!" or "Wow, you're really smart!" Bragging about my accomplishments is fun. But then I read the Bible and see that You're not happy about all my bragging. You want me to take my eyes off my own accomplishments and spend some time building others up. Help me turn my focus off of myself, please! Amen.

─────── THINK ABOUT IT: ───────

Is God proud of you when you learn a new talent
or do well in school? Is He proud of others too?

DOING THE RIGHT THING

Do not let yourselves get tired of doing good. If we do not give up, we will get what is coming to us at the right time.
GALATIANS 6:9

Sometimes doing the right thing is harder than doing the wrong thing, isn't it, Lord God? It's harder to settle down and do my homework than to hang out with my friends or play video games. It's harder to clean my room than to let it stay messy. It's harder to obey my parents when I would rather do my own thing. But Your Word says I need to do the right thing, even when it's tiring. I'm definitely going to need Your help with this! Amen.

THINK ABOUT IT:

What would happen if you always chose to do the wrong thing (the lazy thing)? Would anything ever get done?

YOU ARE FOR ME

What can we say about all these things?
Since God is for us, who can be against us?
ROMANS 8:31

Sometimes it feels like everyone is against me, Lord. The other boys gang up on me. My siblings act like they don't like me. Even my parents don't seem to be on my side sometimes. Then I remember what the Bible says—*You are for me.* That doesn't mean You always think the things I do are right, but You love me even when I mess up. It feels good to know You're on my team, Jesus. Amen.

THINK ABOUT IT:

Being on a team means you work for the whole team, not just yourself. How does it make you feel to know that the Lord is on your team?

WRITTEN IN YOUR BOOK

*Your eyes saw me before I was put together.
And all the days of my life were written in Your
book before any of them came to be.*
PSALM 139:16

Are You writing a book about me, Jesus? Am I a crazy character in the story, or am I a hero? It's amazing to think that You knew how the story would end even before it began. You knew what I would look like—and act like—before I was born. The cool part is, You know what's coming next. I definitely don't, but I'm so glad You do. So I'm learning to trust You with what I cannot see, because I know You've already written the next chapter of my story! Amen.

——— THINK ABOUT IT: ———

Do you totally trust God to write your story?

YOU LIGHT MY WAY

Your Word is a lamp to my feet and a light to my path.
PSALM 119:105

I'm not a big fan of walking in the dark. Sometimes I stub my toe or bump my knee when I get out of bed at night to get a drink of water. It's scary—and painful! I love that Your Word says You are a lamp to my feet and a light to my path. You're always there to guide me when I don't know which way to go. I can fully trust You. You're the best guide ever—better than anyone else! Amen.

───────── **THINK ABOUT IT:** ─────────

If God didn't make things clear to you (which way you should go, which decisions you should make), would you be frozen in place? Aren't You glad He lights the way so you can move forward with confidence?

I WILL NOT HATE

*Why do you try to say your Christian brother is right
or wrong? Why do you hate your Christian brother?
We will all stand before God to be judged by Him.*
ROMANS 14:10

Ugh! Sometimes I get mad, Lord! People hurt me, and I want to hurt them back. They deserve it! (At least I feel like they do.) I feel hate rise up in my heart, and it's not a good feeling. Then I read the Bible and see verses like this one. You don't want me to hate. You don't want me to get even. You don't even want me to judge the other person. This isn't easy! Doing things Your way is *hard*. But I will keep trying with Your help. Amen.

THINK ABOUT IT:

Why does God want you to get rid of any hatred
that is in your heart? Who are you really hurting
when you carry around that kind of hatred?

YOU DON'T MAKE ME AFRAID

*For God did not give us a spirit of fear. He gave us
a spirit of power and of love and of a good mind.*
2 TIMOTHY 1:7

Whenever I'm afraid of something, I must remember
that fear doesn't come from You. You are the opposite
of fear! You teach me to be courageous, to face my
problems with courage that comes from You. You give
me power, love, and good thoughts so I can make the
bravest decisions when hard times come. So I won't
be scared, no matter how rough life gets. I'll just keep
trusting in You, my loving Father! Amen.

———— THINK ABOUT IT: ————

Why do we sometimes forget about the promises
in God's Word when we're going through
tough seasons? Why do we get afraid?

THE RIGHT PATH

*I can have no greater joy than to hear that
my children are following the truth.*
3 JOHN 1:4

Nothing brings You more joy than knowing I'm following after You and living the way Your Word says I should. That brings a smile to Your face, Lord! As I climb into bed tonight, I'm so grateful for Your path. The world has one way of doing things, and You have another. You have placed my feet on the right path. Tomorrow when I wake up, help me to stay on that path and to follow You with every step I take. I want to bring joy to Your heart, Lord! Amen.

—————— THINK ABOUT IT: ——————

Why would an obedient child bring joy
to his parents' hearts? What feelings
would a disobedient child bring?

A SPECIAL PLACE IN YOUR HEART

*But Jesus said, "Let the little children come
to Me. Do not stop them. The holy nation of
heaven is made up of ones like these."*
MATTHEW 19:14

You have a special place in Your heart for children, don't
You, Lord? The Bible says that the kingdom of heaven
is made up of people with childlike faith. Sometimes
I'm not all that kind to the little ones in my life. I lose
my patience with them, especially when they cry. Help
me have Your heart for the children in my life, always
remembering that childlike faith is best. Amen.

——————— THINK ABOUT IT: ———————

What does "childlike faith" mean? Why would
Jesus want us to have the faith of a child?

CHILDREN ARE A REWARD

See, children are a gift from the Lord.
The children born to us are our special reward.
PSALM 127:3

You must really like kids, Jesus. You say that the kingdom of heaven is like children, and You also say that kids are a gift. Some families have lots of kids, so they have a lot of gifts! Some only have one or two. Kids are all different. Some are short, some are tall, some have red hair, some have blond or brown. Some have light skin, some have dark. All of Your "presents" look different, but they are all precious to You! Thank You for reminding me that they should be precious to me too. Amen.

--- **THINK ABOUT IT:** ---

Why do you suppose God made children
look so different from each other?

WHAT PEOPLE LOOK LIKE

So from now on, we do not think about what people are like by looking at them. We even thought about Christ that way one time. But we do not think of Him that way anymore.
2 CORINTHIANS 5:16

Okay, I'll admit it, Lord. . .sometimes I judge people based on how they look. I don't mean to, but it happens. I know a lot of people are that way. I'm so glad You don't judge based on looks. You don't look at a good-looking person and say, "That one has more value!" Nope. You look at everyone the same. You're not worried about things like freckles, hair, clothes, shoes, and stuff like that. You love us because we're Your kids. Amen.

─────── **THINK ABOUT IT:** ───────

If God preferred pretty or handsome people above others, He wouldn't be a very loving Father, would He? Aren't You glad He loves everyone the same?

MY HOPE COMES FROM YOU

*Our hope comes from God. May He fill you with joy
and peace because of your trust in Him. May your
hope grow stronger by the power of the Holy Spirit.*
ROMANS 15:13

Sometimes I put my hope and trust in the wrong things, Lord. I forget You're the one in charge. I think if I'm strong enough or smart enough or tough enough that I can take care of things on my own. Then something happens and I'm reminded that I'm definitely not the one in charge of me. But You are! I can put my hope and trust in You because I know You will never *ever* let me down. Knowing I can trust in You brings so much peace to my heart. Thanks for always giving me hope. Amen.

—————— **THINK ABOUT IT:** ——————

If you were fully in charge of yourself,
what would happen? Could you really fix
all your problems all by yourself?

MY UMBRELLA

*Every word of God has been proven true. He is
a safe-covering to those who trust in Him.*
PROVERBS 30:5

When it's raining outside, I choose to carry an umbrella.
It keeps those raindrops from getting me soaking wet.
In some ways You're like an umbrella from life's storms,
Jesus. You protect me. You shield me. You keep that
storm from doing any damage. You are my safe-covering,
just like this verse says. I can count on You even when
the winds are howling around me. Thanks for covering
me with Your peace, Jesus. Amen.

THINK ABOUT IT:

What if umbrellas had never been invented?
. . . Aren't you glad for the safety God
provides during life's storms?

WITH ALL MY HEART

*Jesus said to him, " 'You must love the Lord
your God with all your heart and with all
your soul and with all your mind.' "*
MATTHEW 22:37

Sometimes I act like I'm interested in stuff when I'm
really not, Jesus. Like in history class when the teacher
is going on and on about a war that happened over a
hundred years ago. I yawn and force my eyes open, but
I'm not really feeling it. Sometimes I get that way in my
relationship with You too. I tell everyone, "Yes, I love
God," but inside I'm not really "feeling" it. Thank You
for the reminder that You want me to commit to this
relationship 100 percent. Amen.

THINK ABOUT IT:

Why doesn't God want you to fake your relationship
with Him? Why does He want your whole heart?

I WILL BE STILL

*Be quiet and know that I am God. I will be honored
among the nations. I will be honored in the earth.*
PSALM 46:10

It's not always easy for me to be still and quiet, Jesus.
I get worked up. I spout off. I speak my mind. I let my
voice get loud. But Your Word says that I should be still
and remember that You are God. When things don't
seem to be going my way, You're still God. You're still
in charge. And I can trust You, even when I don't feel
like I can. Tonight as I climb into bed, I will do my best to
remember that I can trust You. So I will be still. Amen.

—————— THINK ABOUT IT: ——————

Why does God want you to rest in the truth that
He can be trusted? Does it always feel that way?

THE GIFT OF PEACE

*"Peace I leave with you. My peace I give to you.
I do not give peace to you as the world gives.
Do not let your hearts be troubled or afraid."*
JOHN 14:27

I don't always feel peaceful, that's for sure! Sometimes I'm the opposite of peaceful. I get into bed with my thoughts still tumbling from all the chaos of the day. But Your Word says You can give me peace. I don't have to worry about what tomorrow holds. I don't have to toss and turn, fretting over the problem I'm facing. You've got it under control, Jesus. I just need to place my trust in You, even when it's hard. Help me, please! Amen.

———— THINK ABOUT IT: ————

Why do you think God calls peace a gift?
If He has given You this gift, do you use it?

TRUST AND LOVE

This is what He said we must do: Put your trust in the name of His Son, Jesus Christ, and love each other. Christ told us to do this.
1 JOHN 3:23

When I put my trust in You, it's easier to love others, Lord God. Trusting You means I'm not so focused on myself. I'm not always trying to fix everything. When I live like that, I have more time to notice what others are going through. It feels good to turn my attention away from my own stuff for a change. That's one of the joys of trusting You! Amen.

———— THINK ABOUT IT: ————

Are you the kind of person who spends too much time worrying? Doesn't it feel good to know you can trust God?

I'LL KEEP BELIEVING

Never stop praying.
1 THESSALONIANS 5:17

Sometimes I feel like giving up before the miracle comes. I pray and pray. . .and when things don't go my way, I feel like You're not going to come through for me, Lord. I know You're not a genie in a bottle. I can't just ask for any old thing and expect You to grant my wish. But when it comes to the big stuff—like providing for me and my family—I trust You will come through. It's going to happen in Your time, not mine; but I won't give up. I'll keep praying and believing. Amen.

THINK ABOUT IT:

What if you gave up and stopped praying right before the miracle happened? Do you believe God is faithful to do what He says He will do?

WHEN I CAN'T FIGURE IT OUT

*Trust in the Lord with all your heart, and do
not trust in your own understanding.*
PROVERBS 3:5

Sometimes things happen that really confuse me, Lord. I just don't get it. I don't know why some people act the way they do. I don't know why some things are harder than I thought they would be. I don't know why nothing I do seems to work out. Then I remember that You know everything. You can see what's really going on, even when I can't. So when I can't figure it out, I'll go on trusting You, my all-seeing God. You alone know, and that's enough for me. Amen.

—————— **THINK ABOUT IT:** ——————

If you had all the answers to life's
problems, how boring would life be?

YOU ROSE FROM THE GRAVE!

"He is not here! He has risen from the dead as He said He would. Come and see the place where the Lord lay."
MATTHEW 28:6

Sometimes my problems seem super huge to me, Lord. They feel impossible. Then I remember that You sent Your Son, Jesus, to die for my sins. He promised that He would rise from the grave three days later. . . and He did! When the women went to the tomb where He had been buried, He wasn't there! Jesus had come back to life again! I figure if You're big enough to pull off a miracle like that, You can definitely take care of the *little* problems I'm facing! Thanks for being such a big, *big* God! Amen.

——— THINK ABOUT IT: ———

If God can bring the dead to life, surely He
can fix the problems you're facing.

THE WAY TO PRAY

In the same way, the Holy Spirit helps us where we are weak. We do not know how to pray or what we should pray for, but the Holy Spirit prays to God for us with sounds that cannot be put into words.
ROMANS 8:26

Sometimes I don't even know how to pray, Lord. I can't think of the right words. I get so upset about what's going on in my life that I can't think of what to say or how to say it. That's one reason I'm so glad You can understand me even when I can't express myself. Your Spirit helps me in ways I can't even understand. Thank You for "getting" me and helping me when I'm going through a hard time. Amen.

THINK ABOUT IT:

The Spirit of God lives inside of you, and He's helping you every minute of every day. When you don't know how to pray, you can count on Him to say what you can't.

WHERE IS MY TRUST?

"Do not let your heart be troubled. You have put your trust in God, put your trust in Me also."
JOHN 14:1

When I flip the switch on the wall, I trust that the lights will come on. And when my dad turns the key in the car, he trusts that the car will start. When my teacher starts talking, I trust that she knows what she's talking about. All day long I put my trust in things and people. When I get worried and upset, please help me remember that the best place to put my trust is You, Jesus. Your Word says, "Do not let your heart be troubled." When I put my trust in You, I am at peace. Thank You! Amen.

THINK ABOUT IT:

If you flipped the switch on the wall and the lights didn't come on, what would you do? Change the bulb, right? Isn't it wonderful to know that God will never stop working for you?

FISHING FOR MEN

*Jesus said to them, "Follow Me.
I will make you fish for men!"*
Matthew 4:19

Okay, I'll be honest, Jesus—I didn't really understand this verse when I first read it. *Fishing for men?* What does that mean? Now I get it, though! You're saying that I need to be like a fisherman when I spread the good news of what You did for all people. I need to tell the story like a fisherman puts the bait on a hook. Then I cast my line into the water (share the story with people who don't know). Some of them will believe and be saved. Thank You for teaching me how to fish for souls! Amen.

—————— **THINK ABOUT IT:** ——————

If no one ever shared the gospel story,
how would anyone ever know the good
news of what Jesus did for us?

FROM START TO FINISH

"Teach them to do all the things I have told you. And I am with you always, even to the end of the world."
MATTHEW 28:20

It's hard for me to stick with things—like my homework, for instance. I'm always tempted to give up before things are finished. But You promised to stick with us forever, Jesus, not just a few hours or days. I'm so glad You don't give up—on people or situations. You always do exactly what You've said You will do, no matter how long it takes. Thanks for being a great finisher, Lord! Amen.

——— THINK ABOUT IT: ———

How many times have you started a project but not finished it? (Lots, right?) What if God was like that? What if He never finished what He started?

YOUR WORDS ARE PURE

The words of the Lord are pure words. They are like silver that has been made pure seven times in a stove of earth.
PSALM 12:6

My words aren't always pure, Lord. Sometimes I say things that I shouldn't. I speak in anger. I use words that aren't nice. I get a little sarcastic. You're never like that, though. Your words are always kind and good and loving. They're like precious metal—gold or silver. Please teach me to be more like You. I need to speak golden words that build people up, not tear them down. Amen.

THINK ABOUT IT:

When you read the words in red in the New Testament (the words of Jesus), what do you find? His words to us are truly kind and loving. Shouldn't we speak the same way?

TUCKED AWAY IN MY HEART

Your Word have I hid in my heart,
that I may not sin against You.
PSALM 119:11

When I have something important to keep, I put it in a safe place. I don't want to lose it! That's how it is with the words of the Bible. I don't want to lose them (or forget them), so I hide them away in a safe place—my heart. That way they're always close by. When I'm tempted to get angry or say something mean, those words bounce from my heart to my brain, and I'm reminded that You don't want me to speak in an ugly way to others. Your words are filled with life, so I will keep them close! Amen.

THINK ABOUT IT:

If someone gave you a priceless jewel,
what would you do with it? Why?

YOU'RE STILL WORKING ON ME

*I am sure that God Who began the good
work in you will keep on working in you until
the day Jesus Christ comes again.*
PHILIPPIANS 1:6

You never stop, do You, Lord God? You keep working
on me every day of my life. Even today, when I had
some not-so-great moments, You were working in my
heart, growing me into a better version of myself. And
tomorrow You'll keep on working on me. Every day I'm
becoming more and more like You. When people look at
me, I want them to see You—so please keep on working,
even when I mess things up! Amen.

———— THINK ABOUT IT: ————

If a potter stopped working on the bowl he was
shaping, would it ever become a finished bowl?
How is that comparable to God working on you?

YOU GIVE BACK

"Give, and it will be given to you. You will have more than enough. It can be pushed down and shaken together and it will still run over as it is given to you. The way you give to others is the way you will receive in return."
LUKE 6:38

No matter how much I give, You always return it to me, Jesus! Like that time I gave away one of my favorite toys. Or that time my family gave to someone in need, and then the next thing we knew we were getting blessed in return. I like how You do math! You multiply things back to us. It's amazing—and fun! You promise that we'll never have to go without, and I know You're right. I've seen it time and time again. Thanks for pouring out blessings on us, Lord. Amen.

THINK ABOUT IT:

You can't outgive God, but it might be fun to try! Who can you bless today?

YOU MAKE ME WISE

*For the Lord gives wisdom. Much learning and
understanding come from His mouth.*
PROVERBS 2:6

I want to get smarter every day, Lord. That's why I'm studying and going to school, so that I can learn. You give me wisdom that can't be found in schoolbooks. It can only come from knowing You and following Your Word, the Bible. I don't suppose it would make much sense to be book smart unless I was also wise spiritually. So please keep pouring out Your wisdom, Lord. Show me the verses from Your Word that will help me grow. And hold me close to You, no matter what. Whenever I start to wander away from You, pull me back, I pray! Amen.

THINK ABOUT IT:

Why is wisdom more important than book smarts?

IT'S BETTER TO GIVE

"In every way I showed you that by working hard like this we can help those who are weak. We must remember what the Lord Jesus said, 'We are more happy when we give than when we receive.' "
ACTS 20:35

I have to admit, I like to get stuff, Jesus. I really look forward to birthdays and Christmas when I get lots of cool gifts. It's not wrong to like gifts, but it's way more fun to give stuff away. I love to bless others, especially when they're feeling down or going through a rough time. Giving brings a smile to the face of the person who receives my gift. I love seeing that. Is that how You feel when You give good gifts to me? Do You see me smiling? I hope so! Amen.

─────── **THINK ABOUT IT:** ───────

Why do you suppose God says giving
makes us happier than receiving?

YOU ARE GOOD TO EVERYONE

The Lord is good to all. And His loving-kindness is over all His works.
PSALM 145:9

Boy, I have a lot to learn from You, Jesus! Some days I don't treat everyone the same. I'm kinder to some people than others. I'm nice to my friends but mean to my brother. I'm respectful to my teacher but talk back to my dad. It's weird. I don't mean to do these things, but it keeps happening. I really want to be more like You and treat everyone the same. My parents deserve the same respect and kindness I give my teacher. My siblings deserve the same kindness I show my friends. I'm definitely going to need Your help with this! Amen.

THINK ABOUT IT:

If Jesus loves everyone the same (no matter how they act), doesn't He expect the same from you?

THIS BEAUTIFUL PLANET

And God wanted good to come to them, saying, "Give birth to many. Grow in number. Fill the earth and rule over it. Rule over the fish of the sea, over the birds of the sky, and over every living thing that moves on the earth."
GENESIS 1:28

You love us so much, Jesus! You created human beings to oversee the earth—to rule over the fish of the sea and the birds of the sky. You made us caretakers of the plants and the rivers, the mountains and the valleys. (You put a lot of trust in us.) Tonight as I stretch out in my bed, I want to thank You for this beautiful planet that You gave us. I'll do my best to take care of it! Amen.

--------- THINK ABOUT IT: ---------

God could have put the rabbits or the giraffes in charge of the planet, but He chose mankind. Why do you suppose He did that?

YOUR WORDS ARE FOREVER

*"Heaven and earth will pass away,
but My words will not pass away."*
MATTHEW 24:35

Everything I said and did today is over. I can't take my words back. I can't undo the things I did. Tonight I'll fall asleep, and tomorrow I will wake up and start again with new words, new actions, new situations. And by tomorrow night, those words will have faded away too. But when You speak, Lord, Your words last forever! They don't fade away. The words in the Bible are just as true today as they were two thousand years ago. Wow! Those are some powerful words. Now I see why I should pay more attention to them! Amen.

THINK ABOUT IT:

Aren't you glad some of your not-
so-kind words fade away?

YOU LOVED ME FIRST

We love Him because He loved us first.
1 JOHN 4:19

It's so easy to love people who love me first. They treat me well, and I can't help but love them in return. The kind words they speak win me over! You're the same way, Lord Jesus. You've always been kind to me. Some people I know aren't so kind. They speak ugly words over me, so it's hard to treat them in a loving way. But even with the difficult people, I will keep on trying. (You kept right on loving me even when I didn't deserve it, after all!) I know You want me to love others well. Help me, I pray. Amen.

——————— **THINK ABOUT IT:** ———————

How do you know God loves you? Can you point to something He did to prove that love to you?

WE ARE MADE IN YOUR IMAGE

And God made man in His own likeness. In the likeness of God He made him. He made both male and female.
GENESIS 1:27

When I look in the mirror, I see myself staring back, Lord. I see my eyes, my hair, my smile. But Your Word says that I'm created in *Your* image. So when people see me, they see You! I'm reflecting You with everything I say and all that I do. That's why my words and actions need to match the Bible, because people know that I'm a Christian. I don't want to be a hypocrite (someone who says one thing but does another). I want to represent You well! I'll be needing Your help with this, Lord. Amen.

———— THINK ABOUT IT: ————

What if you called yourself a Christian but didn't act like one? What would people think about God?

SECRET WISDOM

*I pray that the great God and Father of our Lord
Jesus Christ may give you the wisdom of His
Spirit. Then you will be able to understand the
secrets about Him as you know Him better.*
EPHESIANS 1:17

Tonight as I fall asleep, I want to ask for something special, Jesus. I don't need any new toys or clothes. I don't need anything I can see or touch. What I really need—what I really want—is to be more like You. Give me Your wisdom, I pray. Help me make wise choices and decisions. Fill me with Your Spirit so that I can understand the deep secrets about You. Help me know and love You more. Amen.

THINK ABOUT IT:

Would you consider yourself wise? What
would happen if you never got any wiser?

I WON'T TURN AWAY

A fool turns away from the strong teaching of his father, but he who remembers the strong words spoken to him is wise.
PROVERBS 15:5

I don't like to get in trouble, Jesus! Every time an adult disciplines me, I feel sick inside. I can't stand that icky feeling. I want their words to be washed away. I want to pretend they didn't happen. But Your Word says I need to pay attention to the not-so-easy-to-hear words that adults speak. Even when I've done something wrong and they correct me, I won't run away from their words. I'll take the discipline. I'll learn from it. Because I know these godly adults are just trying to bring me closer to You. Amen.

———— THINK ABOUT IT: ————

Would you ever learn life's lessons if you were never disciplined? Why or why not?

EVEN WHEN I DON'T GET IT

Trust in the Lord with all your heart, and do not trust in your own understanding. Agree with Him in all your ways, and He will make your paths straight.
PROVERBS 3:5–6

There are so many things I just don't get, Lord. Sometimes life doesn't make sense. Good people pass away. Innocent people are falsely accused. Mean people hurt kind people. But Your Word says I should trust You even when life doesn't make sense. So I won't lean on my own understanding. I'll trust that You are in control and will make all things right in the end. Thank You for helping me grow my trust. Amen.

THINK ABOUT IT:

What does the word *trust* mean? If you put your trust in God, what are you telling Him?

NEVER FEAR, YOU ARE HERE!

*"Do not fear, for I am with you. Do not be afraid,
for I am your God. I will give you strength, and
for sure I will help you. Yes, I will hold you up
with My right hand that is right and good."*
Isaiah 41:10

When I'm alone, sometimes I get scared. But when
someone else comes into the room—an adult or a good
friend—my fears go away. It helps to know I'm not by
myself! Your Word says I'm never alone. You're always
with me. So I have nothing to fear. . .*ever*! You're right
beside me, giving me strength to get through whatever
troubles come my way. Please help me remember that
when fear begins to take over my heart and mind. Amen.

THINK ABOUT IT:

When you're scared and feeling alone,
what makes you feel better?

YOU HAVE TOLD ME

"Have I not told you? Be strong and have strength of heart! Do not be afraid or lose faith. For the Lord your God is with you anywhere you go."
JOSHUA 1:9

Sometimes the adults in my life have to repeat themselves, Lord. They say things, but I'm not really listening. Their words go in one ear and out the other! (I really should do a better job of paying attention!) I don't want You to have to repeat Yourself, Jesus. You've already told me that I should be strong and courageous. You've already told me to have faith, even when things look scary. So I'll do what You say. I won't make You repeat Yourself this time! Amen.

―――――――― **THINK ABOUT IT:** ――――――――

Do you suppose the adults in your life get tired of repeating things like, "Did you clean your room?" or "Didn't I tell you not to fight with your sister?"

YOU ARE GOOD

*Give thanks to the Lord, for He is good,
for His loving-kindness lasts forever.*
PSALM 136:1

I'm not always good, Lord. (You already know this.) Sometimes I do wrong things. I mess up. But You, Lord? You never mess up. Never *ever* in the history of the world have You made a mistake. You've always done the right thing. That's how I know I can trust You! It's hard to trust people who mess up a lot, but with You I never have to worry about that. You are completely trustworthy—every hour of every day. Thank You for that! Amen.

THINK ABOUT IT:

What makes someone worthy of your
trust? Why is Jesus trustworthy?

PUT OUT THE FIRE!

When there is no wood, the fire goes out. Where there is no one telling secret stories about people, arguing stops.
PROVERBS 26:20

It's so hard not to get caught up in gossip, Jesus! I feel like I'm just one person in a long line of people passing the story along. And it grows and grows. The more people who know, the bigger the tale! I like this verse from Proverbs because it reminds me that gossip can stop with me. If I refuse to pass the tale on to someone else, then it comes to an end. Please remind me, when I'm hearing some gossip, that it's not my story to share. Let it end with me! Amen.

————— **THINK ABOUT IT:** —————

If you saw a forest fire, would you put water on it or gasoline? Water, of course! Gossip is like that. Cover it with water, not gasoline!

I WILL STAND UP

*Be wise in the way you live around those who are
not Christians. Make good use of your time.*
COLOSSIANS 4:5

I feel like I stick out like a sore thumb sometimes, Jesus.
I'm super different from some of the other kids. They
don't believe like I do. They don't act like I do. They
make fun of me because I'm a Christian. It's hard to
be different, and it makes me nervous around them. I
don't always speak up for the truth. Then I remember
that You want me to be courageous. Tomorrow when
I wake up, make me brave for the day ahead! I want to
speak the truth, even when it's really hard. Help me,
please! Amen.

———— THINK ABOUT IT: ————

If no one ever spoke up, would anyone
ever know the truth of who Jesus is?

I'M TRYING TO UNDERSTAND

Try to understand other people. Forgive each other.
If you have something against someone, forgive
him. That is the way the Lord forgave you.
COLOSSIANS 3:13

Some people are just hard to understand, Lord. I don't get them. They make no sense to me. How they act, how they talk. . .it's not good. But I'm trying to learn how to live at peace with everyone, even the hard ones. So I will forgive the ones who hurt me. Tonight before I go to sleep, help me to release the ones I've been holding in unforgiveness. I want to have a good night's sleep, so I choose to let go of my unforgiveness once and for all. Amen.

——— THINK ABOUT IT: ———

If you went on holding a grudge for years and years, what would eventually happen?

MY DEBT IS PAID

*Do not owe anyone anything, but love
each other. Whoever loves his neighbor
has done what the Law says to do.*
ROMANS 13:8

I don't like to owe people stuff, Jesus. It's a terrible feeling. I have trouble sleeping because I'm trying to figure out how to pay them back. That's one reason I'm so grateful that Your Son, Jesus, paid the price on the cross for my sins. He took my debt and paid it in full. Jesus said, "No charge, kid! I've taken care of this one for you!" Now all You ask is that I love You and love others, even when they're not nice to me. That's not always easy! But You say I need to love them anyway, so I'll give it my best shot. I don't want to owe anyone, Lord! Amen.

——— THINK ABOUT IT: ———

What if you owed the bank a million dollars but
never paid it back? What would happen?

I WON'T HURT OTHERS

He who goes about talking to hurt people makes secrets known. So do not be with those who talk about others.
PROVERBS 20:19

Words are like a weapon, aren't they, Jesus? Sometimes I shoot them like an arrow out of a bow. My goal is to hurt people with the words I say. (I'm embarrassed even to admit this, but You already know anyway.) You don't want me to use my words as a weapon. Every word out of my mouth should bring life and peace to my friends, family members, teachers, and even strangers. I won't spread gossip, and I won't deliberately hurt others with my words. Please help me with this, Lord. Amen.

———————— THINK ABOUT IT: ————————

Why is it important to think before you speak? What would happen if you just blurted out everything that came to mind?

I WON'T SPREAD TROUBLE

A bad man spreads trouble. One who hurts
people with bad talk separates good friends.
PROVERBS 16:28

I don't want to be one of those people who goes around causing trouble, Lord. Sometimes it's tempting! I get caught up with the wrong crowd. But when I'm in bed at night, thinking back over my day, I feel so sorry for the trouble I caused. The sadness in my mom's face when I talked back to her. The frustration in my teacher's voice when she told me to behave in class. I don't mean to upset these people. Please forgive me and help me do better tomorrow. Amen.

--- **THINK ABOUT IT:** ---

Do troublemakers bring joy to God's
heart, or do they make Him sad?

I WILL SERVE OTHERS

Most of all, have a true love for each other. Love covers many sins. Be happy to have people stay for the night and eat with you. God has given each of you a gift. Use it to help each other. This will show God's loving-favor.
1 PETER 4:8–10

I like to be the boss, Jesus! I want to be the one who's in charge of things. I think I'm the best leader out there. (Okay, I get a little prideful sometimes!) But Your Word says that humbling myself is the better way. You want me to care about others and their needs. I don't always do a very good job of that. Help me pay more attention to what others need. This will help me know how to pray for them. I want to be someone who serves others, but I'm going to need Your help! Amen.

THINK ABOUT IT:

What if people only thought of themselves?
What kind of world would it be?

I WILL HELP OTHERS UP

For if one of them falls, the other can help him up. But it is hard for the one who falls when there is no one to lift him up.
ECCLESIASTES 4:10

It's not fun to go through life alone, is it, Jesus? I'm glad You've surrounded me with people. I've got friends, family members, teachers, neighbors. . .all sorts of people! The Bible says it's good to stick together. If one person is having a down day, the other person can lift them up. I love people like that! They know how to bring a smile to my face or make me laugh, even when I'm having a terrible day! Please help me be that kind of friend to others. Amen.

THINK ABOUT IT:

If you went through a really hard time completely alone, who would crack a joke and make you laugh? Aren't friends and family members the best when you're feeling blue?

WHEN MY FRIENDS ARE DOWN

"Kindness from a friend should be shown to a man without hope, or he might turn away from the fear of the All-powerful."
JOB 6:14

I want to be the kind of friend who notices when others are hurting. Please give me Your heart for them, Jesus. Help me to see what they're going through, even if they don't tell me. And then show me how to be kind in a way that brings hope when they're feeling down. My kindness could very well be the thing that changes everything for my friend. (I know that kind people always make me feel better.) Help me be that kind of friend, Lord. Amen.

THINK ABOUT IT:

What if you were going through a really rough time but no one noticed or cared? How would that make you feel?

BEST FRIENDS

A man who has friends must be a friend, but there
is a friend who stays nearer than a brother.
PROVERBS 18:24

I have a lot of great friends, but there are a few who are really, really close. They're almost like brothers to me. Your Word, the Bible, says it's good to have brother-friends. I can share my troubles with them. They notice when I'm feeling bad. They care when I'm going through a hard time. They're really more like family than friends. Thank You for these special friendships, Lord. Help me be that kind of friend to others, especially those who really, really need a friend. Amen.

THINK ABOUT IT:

Do you have certain friends you're really close to?
Who are they? What makes them extra special?

CAN'T WE ALL JUST GET ALONG?

*See, how good and how pleasing it is for
brothers to live together as one!*
PSALM 133:1

It's no fun when friends are fighting. Nothing hurts
worse than mean words from someone I once called a
close friend. Sometimes I crawl into bed at night and
all I can think about is the argument I had that day. I
don't like that feeling. You want us to get along, to lay
down our arguing and fighting and think of others in a
godly way. When I do that—when I lay down my selfish
desires—I get along with everyone. You love when we
live in unity, Lord. Help me do my best to live peacefully
with others, I pray. Amen.

THINK ABOUT IT:

What if you lived in a family where no
one ever got along? How awkward and
uncomfortable would that be?

I RESPECT OTHERS

Love each other as Christian brothers.
Show respect for each other.
ROMANS 12:10

Your Word says we should show respect to one another. That means I must treat my friends with honor and kindness, because they deserve it. They are human beings created in Your image and loved by You. If You care about them so much, I need to as well! It's not always easy to respect people, especially the ones who don't treat me well. I'm definitely going to need Your help with some of the not-so-nice people! Show me how to love as You love, even when it's hard. Amen.

THINK ABOUT IT:

What if no one respected you? What if no one treated you kindly? Would it change your life for the better or for the worse?

I WON'T BLAB ABOUT IT

He who covers a sin looks for love. He who tells of trouble separates good friends.
PROVERBS 17:9

My friend messed up, Lord God. You saw it, I'm sure. He did something pretty bad. And I know all about it. His parents know too, and now he's in trouble. I'm tempted to blab to my other friends so that they know what happened. But I won't. Your Word says that I can cover his sin with my love. The Bible also says if I blab, then I'll probably end up separating friends. So I will let you deal with him in Your own way. It's not my place to fix this situation. That's Your job. Amen.

———— THINK ABOUT IT: ————

How would you feel if you messed up and your good friend blabbed about it to others?

I AM A LIGHT

"You are the light of the world. You cannot hide a city that is on a mountain. Men do not light a lamp and put it under a basket. They put it on a table so it gives light to all in the house. Let your light shine in front of men. Then they will see the good things you do and will honor your Father Who is in heaven."
MATTHEW 5:14–16

When I gave my heart to You, You placed Your light in me, Jesus. Now You want me to shine for everyone to see. I will do my best to be a good witness for You so that other people can come to know You. When they do, You will turn on the light inside of them too! In this way, more and more people throughout the whole world will be shining bright for You! Amen.

———— THINK ABOUT IT: ————

What if you didn't shine your light? Would others know about Jesus? It's time to shine bright!

I WILL LEARN FROM MY MISTAKES

Listen to words about what you should do, and take your punishment if you need it, so that you may be wise the rest of your days.
PROVERBS 19:20

I don't always get it right, Jesus. Sometimes (like today) I mess up. When I get into bed at night, I feel bad about some of the things I said and did, especially if it upset my parents. So before I go to sleep, I want to ask for Your forgiveness. I don't like being disciplined, but I want to learn from my mistakes so that I don't make them again. Help me start fresh tomorrow. Amen.

--------- **THINK ABOUT IT:** ---------

Does anyone like to be disciplined? Why does the Bible say it's important to take your punishment so that you can be wise? What does that mean, exactly?

I WILL PUT OTHERS FIRST

*Then give me true joy by thinking the
same thoughts. Keep having the same love.
Be as one in thoughts and actions.*
PHILIPPIANS 2:2

Putting others first isn't usually how I live, Lord. Most of the time it's me, myself, and I. I usually just want what I want, and I keep arguing with my parents until they say yes or I decide to give up. But Your Word says I need to be others-focused. I need to take care of the needs of people, like that kid at school who doesn't have lunch money. And that elderly neighbor who needs help around the house. There are a ton of things I can do if I really think about it. Give me creative ideas, Lord. Amen.

———— THINK ABOUT IT: ————

In what fun and creative ways can you bless
others tomorrow? Who needs your help?

WHO SHOULD I HANG OUT WITH?

He who walks with wise men will be wise, but the one who walks with fools will be destroyed.
PROVERBS 13:20

Sometimes it's hard to know who to hang out with, Lord. After I meet new kids who seem cool, I start spending time with them. Only, sometimes I find out too late that they're not as cool as I thought. They're secretly doing stuff they shouldn't. I get drawn into these relationships, and I'm scared to walk away. Thank You for the reminder that I should be walking with wise people, not foolish ones. Help me do the right thing, Lord Jesus. Amen.

THINK ABOUT IT:

Are you hanging out with someone who's pulling you away from God? What should you do about it?

I AM WHO I SAY I AM

*If a person says, "I love God," but hates his
brother, he is a liar. If a person does not
love his brother whom he has seen, how can
he love God Whom he has not seen?*
1 John 4:20

Sometimes I pretend to be something—or someone—I'm
not, Lord. Like, I'll say something nice to someone to
their face, but behind their back I say something completely different. I'm a faker sometimes. I'm so sorry. I
don't mean to be this way. I don't want to be a hypocrite
(someone who says one thing but does another). Help
me be who I say I am. I know this is super important
to You. I'm definitely going to need Your help! Amen.

THINK ABOUT IT:

Do you ever find yourself being kind to someone to
their face but mean behind their back? How would
you feel if your friends were like this to you?

I'M THANKFUL FOR MY BODY

*I will give thanks to You, for the greatness of
the way I was made brings fear. Your works
are great and my soul knows it very well.*
PSALM 139:14

Sometimes I look in the mirror and don't like what I see,
Lord. I don't like my hair. Or my nose. Or how short I am.
I moan and groan about how I wish I could look like some
of the other boys. Then I remember that You created
me just the way I am, and You think I'm amazing! Tonight
as I sleep, please help me rest in Your truth—that what
I look like on the outside isn't what's important to You.
It's what's on the inside that counts. Amen.

THINK ABOUT IT:

Who created you to look like you do? If God
made those decisions—about your hair, skin,
size, and shape—who are you to argue with
Him? Learn to love yourself as He loves you.

IT'S EASY TO OBEY YOU, JESUS!

Loving God means to obey His Word,
and His Word is not hard to obey.
1 JOHN 5:3

I always act like it's such a big deal to obey, like it's *way* too hard. But when it comes to following the Bible, it's really not that hard. I just have to learn to love You first and then love others as I love myself. If I can do those things, the rest will come naturally. I won't have to worry about anger or jealousy or other problems like that if I'm really walking in Your ways. Help me to grow stronger and stronger in You and to live by Your Word, Jesus. Amen.

———— THINK ABOUT IT: ————

If you were playing a sport, you would follow a rulebook, right? (Every sport has rules!) What would happen if you didn't follow the rulebook? You wouldn't win many games, would you?

I WANT TO BE A GOOD FINISHER

*I have fought a good fight. I have finished the
work I was to do. I have kept the faith.*
2 TIMOTHY 4:7

I want to be a guy who finishes well, Jesus. Sometimes
I start stuff—like a good book or a puzzle—and I give
up before finishing. Other times I start working on a
homework assignment but get distracted. And sometimes (just being honest) I start cleaning my room but
give up before I get it cleaned. (Hey, there's a lot of
cool stuff in my room to distract me!) You care as much
about my finishes as my starts, so please help me do
better tomorrow. Amen.

THINK ABOUT IT:

What if God had started creating the world,
only to get distracted when He got to the
zebras? He finishes well, and you should too!

I WILL DO IT YOUR WAY

*How can a young man keep his way
pure? By living by Your Word.*
PSALM 119:9

I love when I get to make the rules, Lord. I like being the boss. But I'm learning that sometimes when I follow my own path, I get off course. I end up doing things that aren't good. In other words, my way isn't the best way. You have a better way, and it's found in Your Word. If I follow it like a map, I will end up going exactly where You want me to go. I won't get lost along the way. So tonight as I climb into bed, I'm laying down my desire to always get my way. It won't be easy, but it will be totally worth it! Amen.

THINK ABOUT IT:

What if you always got your way? Would that
leave any room for others to have their way
too? How sad the world would be if we all
followed our own path and left God out!

YOUR WORKS ARE GREAT!

I will give thanks to You, for the greatness of the way I was made brings fear. Your works are great and my soul knows it very well.
PSALM 139:14

I love to make stuff. Hobby projects. Crafts. It's fun to work with my hands and create things. Most of the stuff I make is okay. . .not great. But everything You make, Lord? It's all perfect! Like the earth and everything in it—rivers, mountains, lakes, animals, flowers, and all sorts of colorful things. You are literally perfect! You even thought of everything when You made me. You gave me eyes to see, a mouth to speak, a nose to breathe, hands to use, feet to move. . .and everything else I could ever need. Your works are truly great! Amen.

THINK ABOUT IT:

What if God had given you only one eye or one ear? What if He had given you three feet or four arms?

ALL THINGS ARE POSSIBLE

Jesus looked at them and said, "This cannot be done by men. But with God all things can be done."
MATTHEW 19:26

Sometimes I wish I had superhero powers. I wish I could fly. I wish I could blink my eyes and be transported from one place to another. (That would be so cool!) But I'm limited. A lot of things are impossible for humans to do! Then I remember that nothing is impossible for You. . .absolutely *nothing*! You can make miracles happen! You parted the Red Sea and saved the Israelites from their enemies. You heal people who are sick. You help people overcome anger and other issues. You can do everything, Lord! Amen.

THINK ABOUT IT:

Can you think of one thing that God can't do?

I WILL ALWAYS LOOK TO YOU

*Look to the Lord and ask for His
strength. Look to Him all the time.*
1 CHRONICLES 16:11

People give me all kinds of advice. Some people tell me to do one thing. Other people tell me to do another. I get confused with all the opinions! That's why I'm so glad I have You, Lord. Right now, in the quiet of my bedroom, I'll crawl into bed and think about the decisions I have to make. I'll think about the suggestions others have made. But then I'll ask Your opinion. (That's what matters most to me, after all.) I'm looking to You for answers, Lord. I'm looking to You for strength. Amen.

THINK ABOUT IT:

Of all the people you trust,
who gives the best advice?

THE HEART OF A LION

The sinful run away when no one is trying to catch them, but those who are right with God have as much strength of heart as a lion.
PROVERBS 28:1

When I'm right with You—when I follow Your Word and live a godly life—my heart is as strong as a lion's. Wow, Lord! That's pretty strong! I don't have to run for my life when my heart is right with You. You keep me safe and secure. I can rest easy. And You make me brave, even when the enemy tries to take me down. With You on my side, I can't lose! Thanks for guarding my heart and making me strong. Amen.

THINK ABOUT IT:

Is a lion fearful about every little thing?
Of course not! He's the king of the jungle.
Doesn't God make you brave and strong
like a lion when you walk with Him?

ACTIONS SPEAK LOUDER THAN WORDS

My children, let us not love with words or in talk only. Let us love by what we do and in truth.
1 JOHN 3:18

I've heard adults say this before: Actions speak louder than words. Sometimes I forget, Jesus. Mom will say, "Go clean your room," and I'll respond with, "Okay." But then I forget to do what I said I would do. I get distracted by a video game controller I found under the bed. And before long, I'm playing video games. My room never gets clean. Then my mom comes in to check on me, sees the mess, and gets upset. I don't blame her, Lord. My actions speak *a lot* louder than my words. You want me to follow through, but I'll need Your help! Amen.

—————— **THINK ABOUT IT:** ——————

What if no one ever did what
they said they would do?

JEALOUSY HAS A BAD ENDING

*Wherever you find jealousy and fighting, there will
be trouble and every other kind of wrong-doing.*
JAMES 3:16

I read a lot of books, and some don't have great endings,
Jesus. I wish they would end differently. That's kind of
how it is when people get jealous. Their story doesn't
end well. Instead of a happy ending, they end up fighting
and arguing. (That's not good!) You say to stay away
from envy (jealousy) so that my story can end well. I'm
doing my best, Lord. Amen.

─────────── THINK ABOUT IT: ───────────

Do you ever think about how your story
will end? What if you put away jealousy
and spent your time loving others?

LEGACY

Grandchildren are the pride and joy of old men and a son is proud of his father.
PROVERBS 17:6

I never really thought much about this word *legacy*, Lord. I didn't understand what it meant. Now I get it: a legacy is something passed down from one generation to another. My grandparents left a legacy to my parents, and my parents will leave one to me. I'm so glad I get to be part of their family. I'm part of a long line of people from one big family tree. I want to live in a way that makes them proud to call me their own. And one day, I hope to pass on that legacy to the ones who will come after me. Help me live a good life so I can do that, Lord. Amen.

THINK ABOUT IT:

You have parents. Your parents have parents. Their parents had parents. And so on. Your family legacy goes w-a-y back multiple generations. How can you live in a way that honors all of them?

IT MATTERS TO YOU

Do as God would do. Much-loved children want to do as their fathers do. Live with love as Christ loved you. He gave Himself for us, a gift on the altar to God which was as a sweet smell to God.
EPHESIANS 5:1–2

Are you really watching every move I make, Jesus? I get a little embarrassed thinking about it, especially when I make mistakes (like not treating someone nicely). You're watching how I treat the kids that no one else seems to notice—the boy in the wheelchair, the kids in special ed, that one girl who is absent from school a lot because she's always sick. You care about every single person, and you want me to care as well. Help me become a difference-maker, Jesus. Amen.

THINK ABOUT IT:

If something matters to God,
shouldn't it matter to you too?

SUCH A GOOD FATHER

Of what great worth is Your loving-kindness, O God!
The children of men come and are safe in the shadow
of Your wings. They are filled with the riches of Your
house. And You give them a drink from Your river of joy.
PSALM 36:7–8

Not all the fathers I know are good, Lord. I know some adults who yell and swear and do other bad things. They don't always treat their kids well. But You? You're the very best kind of Father! You shower Your kids with love and blessings. You're like a mother hen, gathering her chicks under her wings. We're safe in the shadow of Your wings. You provide for us, teach us, and use us to reach others with the gospel message—and You go right on loving us even when we mess up. You truly are a good, good Father! Amen.

—————— **THINK ABOUT IT:** ——————

What words would you use to describe God?

YOU ARE FIGHTING FOR ME

But Moses said to the people, "Do not be afraid!
Be strong, and see how the Lord will save you
today. For the Egyptians you have seen today,
you will never see again. The Lord will fight
for you. All you have to do is keep still."
EXODUS 14:13–14

I remember watching my friend get beat up by a bully,
Lord. Then, right in the middle of the fight, my friend's
older brother showed up. That bully took off in a hurry!
The older brother chased him off and said, "Don't ever
mess with my brother again!" And he didn't. That's what
it's like with You on my side. You tell the enemy, "Hey,
he's My kid! Don't mess with him!" And the devil takes
off running! You do the fighting. I do the resting. I'll be
still and watch You fight for me. Thanks, Lord! Amen.

THINK ABOUT IT:

Did you ever think about God fighting before
you read this verse? What does God ask of you
while He's doing the fighting? (Hint: Be still!)

BLESSING AND CURSING

Giving thanks and speaking bad words come from the same mouth. My Christian brothers, this is not right! Does a well of water give good water and bad water from the same place?
JAMES 3:10–11

Oops. I did it again. The same mouth that speaks praises and blessings just slipped up and said something bad. You tell me in Your Word that I shouldn't let blessing and cursing come from the same mouth. I need to back away from harsh, ugly words and speak only kind, loving ones. A well doesn't give both good water and bad. My mouth shouldn't give good speech and bad either. Help me, please. I want to do better. Amen.

THINK ABOUT IT:

How is your mouth like a well of water?

YOU'RE WAITING FOR ME

The Lord is not slow about keeping His promise as some people think. He is waiting for you. The Lord does not want any person to be punished forever. He wants all people to be sorry for their sins and turn from them.
2 PETER 3:9

I don't like to keep people waiting, Jesus. I don't want to be the reason we're late! It happens sometimes, but it's always embarrassing when it does. I especially don't want to keep You waiting! If You ask me to do something, I want to do it right away. You ask me to say I'm sorry right away when I've hurt someone (or hurt You), and I want to do so quickly! Please forgive me for the times I kept You waiting. Amen.

──────── **THINK ABOUT IT:** ────────

God always keeps His promises to you.
Do you always keep your promises to Him?

YOU GIVE ME REST

"Come to Me, all of you who work and have heavy loads. I will give you rest. Follow My teachings and learn from Me. I am gentle and do not have pride. You will have rest for your souls. For My way of carrying a load is easy and My load is not heavy."
MATTHEW 11:28–30

My life is so crazy busy sometimes, Lord! There's just so much to do. School. Chores. Family stuff. Church stuff. Sports. I'm up to my eyeballs in activities. Sometimes it gets so overwhelming that I just want to quit all of it. It feels like too much to carry. You tell me that You can give me rest if I will just bring my problems to You. So that's what I'm doing tonight. I won't stress. Instead, I'll come to You. Thanks for giving me rest. Amen.

———— THINK ABOUT IT: ————

What if you never paused from your busyness long enough to lay your problems down at God's feet? What would happen?

HOW TO TREAT TROUBLEMAKERS

*Pray and give thanks for those who make
trouble for you. Yes, pray for them instead of
talking against them. Be happy with those who
are happy. Be sad with those who are sad.*
ROMANS 12:14–15

You know me, Jesus. I get super mad at people sometimes! I just want to get even with them when they hurt me. (That's fair, right?) Only, You say *no*. You have a different plan. You want me to adjust my attitude before demanding that others change. That's hard! I definitely need an attitude adjustment. Instead of getting cranky when people cause trouble, I need to follow the advice in this scripture and pray that good things will happen to them. Tonight I'm asking You to change my thinking so I'm more like You. Amen.

─────── **THINK ABOUT IT:** ───────

Who is the biggest troublemaker you know? What can you do to change your thinking about him or her?

A CUP OF COLD WATER

"For sure, I tell you, anyone who gives a cup of cold water to one of these little ones because he follows Me, will not lose his reward."
MATTHEW 10:42

You ask me to do the simple things, Jesus. Things like giving someone a cup of cold water when they're thirsty. (That's pretty simple!) Sometimes these simple acts of kindness say a lot. When a person is feeling lonely or down in the dumps, a kind act will bring a smile. And it's definitely not hard for me to pay attention to the ones who need a kind word or deed. Thanks for reminding me that I can change someone's life with one simple act! Amen.

—————— THINK ABOUT IT: ——————

Do you know anyone who's been down in the dumps lately? What simple thing can you do to help lift their spirits?

EVERYTHING GOOD COMES FROM YOU

Whatever is good and perfect comes to us from God. He is the One Who made all light. He does not change. No shadow is made by His turning.
JAMES 1:17

All the good things I see come from You, Jesus. You made the earth and everything in it. You created stars to twinkle in the sky. You made the sun, the moon, the earth and other planets. You thought of everything—rushing rivers, snowcapped mountains, even beautiful stretches of farmland. You made fish in the sea, birds in the air, and puppies that chase their own tails. You decided the world needed a kid like me, so You made me too. All Your gifts are wonderful! Amen.

THINK ABOUT IT:

If God made the good things, then who caused the bad things? Why shouldn't we blame God for the bad stuff?

I WILL PROVE IT BY MY ACTIONS

*A young man makes himself known by his actions and
proves if his ways are pure and right. The hearing ear
and the seeing eye were both made by the Lord.*
PROVERBS 20:11–12

Jesus, I've heard adults say things like, "If you really
mean what you say, then prove it with your actions."
They want me to follow through and actually do what
I've said I will do. (I'm not always the best at this, to be
honest. Sometimes I say things, but I don't do them.)
Your Word says that I can prove that my actions are pure
if I just do the right things. I want to prove to others
that I am who I say I am. May I prove my words with
my actions. Amen.

——— THINK ABOUT IT: ———

They say that actions speak louder than words.
Do you think this is true? Why do people say this?

SET APART

Your heart should be holy and set apart for
the Lord God. Always be ready to tell everyone
who asks you why you believe as you do.
Be gentle as you speak and show respect.
1 PETER 3:15

You want me to be different than other people, don't You, Jesus? I'm not supposed to go along with the crowd. I've been set apart to do great things for You. That's why it's so important that I guard what I say and do. It's why I can't overreact to every little thing—because I'm representing You. When people ask me, "Why are you always smiling?" I will say, "It's because of Jesus!" Thank You for making me Your child. Amen.

THINK ABOUT IT:

God chose you! He picked you to be different. You're so special to Him. Why is it important that you represent Him well?

A PURE HEART

*Keep your heart pure for out of it are
the important things of life.*
Proverbs 4:23

You want me to keep my heart pure, Lord. It's not always easy. Sometimes I hang around kids who are the opposite of pure. They say not-so-great things. They have a temper. They do wrong things. And the more I hang around them, the more like them I become. Help me to keep my heart pure so I can represent You well. If I stay pure, great things will come out of my heart, and others will see that I follow You. I'll definitely need Your help with this! Amen.

THINK ABOUT IT:

If you poured fresh water into a dirty
cup, what would happen? Would you feel
comfortable drinking that water?

A WISE GUY

*Do not be wise in your own eyes. Fear the
Lord and turn away from what is sinful.*
PROVERBS 3:7

Sometimes I think I'm the smartest one in the room. I
brag on myself. I think I have all the answers. But You
say I shouldn't act this way. I'm not supposed to be wise
in my own eyes. Instead of focusing on how great I am,
I need to draw attention away from myself and toward
You. You're the one who's wise, Lord. You're the one
who can help me turn away from my mistakes. Thanks
for guiding me. Amen.

THINK ABOUT IT:

Do you ever feel like you're smarter (or
wiser) than everyone else? What happens
when you start feeling that way?

GENTLENESS

They must not speak bad of anyone, and they must not argue. They should be gentle and kind to all people.
Titus 3:2

I'm not always gentle, Lord Jesus. Sometimes I'm a little harsh! I blow up at people and then regret it. I make fast decisions that aren't always wise. I get a little bossy. I don't want to be like this. I know that Jesus-followers are meant to be gentle and kind to everyone. (Why is that always hardest with the people I love the most?) Help me, please. I want to be more like You—gentle, caring, and patient with others. Amen.

THINK ABOUT IT:

Is Jesus gentle with you? When was the last time He treated you gently when you probably deserved discipline?

IT MATTERS TO YOU

The Lord tests and proves those who are right
and good and those who are sinful. And His
soul hates the one who loves to hurt others.
PSALM 11:5

Are You watching my every move, Jesus? Do you really see when I mess up or treat others badly? I can do a better job! Help me to notice the kids others ignore. You care about every single one of them, Jesus, and so should I! You smile when I take the time to care for those who are less fortunate than I am, because You want me to make a difference and show everyone that they matter. Thanks for the reminder, Lord. Amen.

THINK ABOUT IT:

Are there any kids in school you have overlooked? What can you do to let them know they are noticed?

WAITING FOR MY CROWN

*Everyone who runs in a race does many things
so his body will be strong. He does it to get a
crown that will soon be worth nothing, but we
work for a crown that will last forever.*
1 CORINTHIANS 9:25

Life is hard, and sometimes I feel like giving up, Jesus.
That's especially true some nights when I climb into
bed. I just want to pull the covers over my head and
say, "Enough!" I don't always feel like waking up the
next morning to the same crazy life. But You say that
I need to keep running the race, so I will. I'm getting
stronger and stronger, the more problems I face. And
one day You'll give me a crown and say, "Good job!
Race well run!" So I'll keep going, even when I don't
feel like it. Amen.

THINK ABOUT IT:

What if Jesus hadn't finished His race? What if
He gave up before dying for your sins? Aren't
you glad He ran all the way to the finish line?

SCRIPTURE INDEX

The Old Testament

The New Testament

MORE BEDTIME BIBLE INSPIRATION FOR KIDS!

365 Classic Bedtime Bible Stories

Beginning with the creation story, "God Creates the Earth," and ending with "In Eternity with God," your children will develop faith in an almighty God who is the same yesterday, today, and forever, while journeying alongside Bible characters like Samuel, Jonah, Esther, David, John the Baptist, Mary, Joseph, and many more. *365 Classic Bedtime Bible Stories* promises to make bedtime reading a delightful learning and faith-building experience!

Hardback / 978-1-63058-380-4